*for work and play*

# JACKETS

**theBestofKnitter's**

*a publication of*  BOOKS

PUBLISHER
Alexis Yiorgos Xenakis

COEDITORS
Rick Mondragon
Elaine Rowley

EDITORIAL ASSISTANTS
Jennifer Dyke
Sue Kay Nelson

INSTRUCTION EDITOR
Joni Coniglio

INSTRUCTION ASSISTANTS
Traci Bunkers
Mary Lou Eastman
Kelly Rokke
Carol Thompson

COPYEDITOR
Wendy Siera

GRAPHIC DESIGNER
Bob Natz

PHOTOGRAPHER
Alexis Xenakis

SECOND PHOTOGRAPHER
Mike Winkleman

DIRECTOR, PUBLISHING SERVICES
David Xenakis

STYLISTS
Lisa Mannes
Rick Mondragon

TECHNICAL ILLUSTRATOR
Carol Skallerud

PRODUCTION DIRECTOR & COLOR SPECIALIST
Dennis Pearson

BOOK PRODUCTION MANAGER
Greg Hoogeveen

DIGITAL PREPRESS
Everett Baker
Nancy Holzer
Jay Reeve

MIS
Jason Bittner

FIRST PUBLISHED IN THE USA IN 2006 BY XRX, INC.

ISBN 1-933064-05-6
Produced in Sioux Falls, South Dakota, by XRX, Inc.,
PO Box 1525, Sioux Falls, SD 57101-1525 USA 605.338.2450

a publication of XX BOOKS

visit us online knittinguniverse.com XX

# *for work and play*
# JACKETS

photography by
**Alexis Xenakis**

*a publication of* XRX *BOOKS*

# contents

XOX BOOKS

# welcome

A jacket is the final layer of dress that can define our look—not just by shape and silhouette but by fabrication as well.

And a knit jacket offers even more. Personalize yours with color, length, and trim. Choose to knit one that is refined, polished, and tailored for work or one that is more casual, soft, and relaxed for play.

Throughout this book, the yarns are described generically and the specific yarn is listed with each photograph. Some of the yarns are no longer available, but may live on in our memories and stashes.

You'll find projects with interesting details and stitch patterns that are fun to knit. But best of all, you'll end up with jackets that mean business.

# work & play

Lana Hames

*Horizontal welts and vertical ribs of knit and purl weave this wonderfully textured fabric.*

# beautiful basket stitchery

**INTERMEDIATE**

STANDARD FIT

**Sizes XS (S, M, L, 1X, 2X)**
**Shown in Small**
A 35½ (38½, 41½, 47½, 53½, 56½)"
B 20½ (21½, 23½, 25, 26, 27)"
C 27 (28, 28½, 29½, 31, 31½)"

10cm/4"

32 ▦

24

• over chart pattern (slightly stretched) using larger needles

1 2 **3** 4 5 6

• **Light weight**
• 1425 (1605, 1835, 2140, 2430, 2610) yds

• 3.75mm/US 5 and 4.5mm/US 7, or size to obtain gauge, 60cm/24" long

• 7 (7, 8, 8, 9, 9) 25mm/1"

• stitch holders
• stitch markers

**original yarn**
RUSSI SALES Heirloom Easy Care 8 (wool; 50g; 107 yds) Teal

## Notes

**1** See *School*, page 94 for 3-needle bind-off. **2** Sweater is knit in one piece to underarm, then divided for fronts and back.

## Body

With smaller needle, cast on 208 (226, 244, 280, 316, 334) stitches. Work Chart pattern for 8 rows. Change to larger needle. Continue to work chart pattern until piece measures 13½ (13½, 15, 15½, 16, 16½)" from beginning, end with a WS row.
*Divide for fronts and back*
**Next row** (RS) Work 45 (50, 54, 62, 70, 74) stitches (right front), bind off 9 (8, 9, 9, 13, 14) stitches (underarm), work until there are 100 (110, 118, 138, 150, 158) stitches for back, bind off 9 (8, 9, 9, 13, 14) stitches (underarm), work to end (left front). **Next row** (WS) Work 45 (50, 54, 62, 70, 74) stitches of left front and place remaining stitches on hold.

## Left Front

*Shape armhole*
Continue pattern, bind off at armhole edge (beginning of RS rows) 2 (2, 2, 3, 3, 3) stitches twice—41 (46, 50, 56, 64, 68) stitches. Work even until armhole measures 6 (7, 7½, 8½, 9, 9½)", end with a RS row.
*Shape neck*
**Next row** (WS) Bind off 8 (10, 12, 12, 14, 16) stitches (neck edge), work to end. Continue to bind off at neck edge (beginning of WS rows) 2 stitches twice—29 (32, 34, 40, 46, 48) stitches. Work even until armhole measures 7 (8, 8½, 9½, 10, 10½)". Place stitches on hold.

## Right Front

With WS facing, join yarn at underarm edge and work as for left front, reversing shaping by binding off armhole stitches at beginning of WS rows, and neck stitches at beginning of RS rows.

## Back

With WS facing, join yarn at underarm edge and shape armholes as for fronts—92 (102, 110, 126, 138, 146) stitches. Work even until armhole measures same length as fronts to shoulder. Place stitches on hold.

## Sleeves

With smaller needle, cast on 46 (46, 55, 55, 55, 55) stitches. **Begin Chart pattern: Row 1** (RS) Work 18-stitch repeat 2 (2, 3, 3, 3, 3) times, work next 10 (10, 1, 1, 1, 1) stitches of chart. Work 7 rows more in chart pattern as established. Change to larger needle. Continue in chart pattern, AT SAME TIME, increase 1 stitch each side (working increases into pattern) on next row, then every 6th (4th, 4th, 4th, 2nd, 2nd) row 14 (12, 9, 30, 8, 14) times, then every 8th (6th, 6th, 6th, 4th, 4th) row 6

(14, 16, 2, 29, 26) times—88 (100, 107, 121, 131, 137) stitches. Work even until piece measures 18½" from beginning, end with a WS row.
*Shape cap*
Bind off 4 (4, 4, 5, 6, 7) stitches at beginning of next 2 rows, 2 (2, 2, 3, 3, 3) stitches at beginning of next 4 rows. Bind off remaining 72 (84, 91, 99, 107, 111) stitches.

## Finishing

Block pieces. Join shoulders, using 3-needle bind-off, as follows: Join 29 (32, 34, 40, 46, 48) stitches of first shoulder, bind off back neck stitches until 29 (32, 34, 40, 46, 48) stitches remain, then join second shoulder.
*Buttonband*
With RS facing and smaller needle, pick up and knit 110 (116, 128, 137, 143, 149) stitches along left front edge. **Row 1** (WS) Knit. **Rows 2 and 3** Purl. **Rows 4 and 5** Knit. **Rows 6–9** Repeat Rows 2–5. **Row 10** Purl. Bind off knitwise.
*Buttonhole band*
Mark positions for 7 (7, 8, 8, 9, 9) buttonholes along right front edge, with the first ½" from neck edge, the last ¾" from lower edge, and 5 (5, 6, 6, 7, 7) others spaced evenly between. Work as for buttonband, working buttonholes at markers on Row 5 as follows: bind off 3 stitches for each buttonhole; on following row, cast on 3 stitches over bound-off stitches.
*Collar*
With RS facing and smaller needle, beginning at right front neck edge (excluding buttonhole band), pick up and knit 15 (17, 19, 19, 21, 23) stitches to shoulder, 34 (38, 42, 46, 46, 50) stitches along back neck, and 15 (17, 19, 19, 21, 23) stitches along left neck edge to buttonband—64 (72, 80, 84, 88, 96) stitches. **Rows 1 and 2** Purl. **Rows 3 and 4** Knit. **Rows 5-32** Repeat rows 1-4 seven times. **Rows 33 and 34** Repeat Rows 1 and 2. Cut yarn. With WS of sweater facing and using end of needle from right front, pick up and purl 5 stitches along top of buttonband, then pick up and knit 19 stitches along side edge of collar, knit across collar stitches, pick up and knit 19 stitches along side edge of collar, pick up and purl 5 stitches along top of buttonhole band. Bind off knitwise. Set in sleeves. Sew sleeve seams. Sew on buttons.

## Sleeve

14½ (16½, 17½, 20, 21½, 22½)"

¾"

18½ "

7¾ (7¾, 9, 9, 9, 9)"

5¾ (6¼, 7, 7¾, 7¾, 8¼)"     4¾ (5¼, 5¾, 6¾, 7¾, 8)"

1"

**Left Front**     **Back**     **Right Front**

7 (8, 8½, 9½, 10, 10½)"

13½ (13½, 15, 15½, 16, 16½)"

19½ (20½, 22½, 24, 25, 26)"

34½ (37½, 40½, 46½, 52½, 55½)"

### Stitch key
☐ Knit on RS, purl on WS
▨ Purl on RS, knit on WS

### Chart Pattern

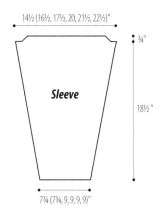

18-st repeat

*Tailored details give this simplest of jackets a professional look. A smooth yarn defines the stitch pattern. The choice of buttons and trim color gives the jacket a personal finish.*

# charcoal strategy

**INTERMEDIATE**

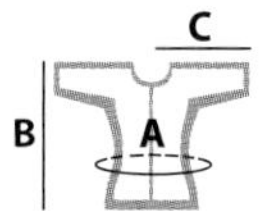

**STANDARD FIT**

**Sizes S (M, L, 1X)**
**Shown in Medium**
A 37¾ (41¼, 44½, 47½)"
B 21 (22, 22½, 23½)"
C 29½ (30½, 31, 32)"

**10cm/4"**

34
20
• over seed stitch,
using larger needles

1 2 3 **4** 5 6

• Medium weight
MC • 1495 (1650, 1790, 1960) yds
CC • 185 (195, 205, 215) yds

• 4mm/US 6 and 4.5mm/US 7,
or size to obtain gauge

• 4mm/US 6, 74cm/29" long

• ten 19mm/¾"

• stitch holders

**original yarn**
PATONS Classic wool (wool; 100g;
223 yds) charcoal (MC), black (CC)
Reknit in BERROCO Ultra Alpaca
(alpaca; wool; 100g; 215 yds)
sweet potato (MC) and black (CC)

## Seed stitch (over an odd number of stitches)
*Row 1* (RS) * K1, p1; repeat from * end k1. *Row 2* Knit the purl stitches and purl the knit stitches. Repeat row 2 for seed stitch.

## Back
With larger needles and MC, cast on 91 (99, 107, 115) stitches. Work in seed stitch for 16 rows. Cast on 2 stitches at beginning of next 2 rows—95 (103, 111, 119) stitches. Continue in seed stitch until piece measures 11 (11½, 11½, 12)" from beginning, end with a WS row.
*Shape armholes*
Bind off 4 stitches at beginning of next 2 rows. Decrease 1 stitch each side every row 3 (3, 5, 7) times, then every other row 1 (3, 3, 3) times—79 (83, 87, 91) stitches. Work even until armhole measures 9 (9½, 10, 10½)", end with a WS row.
*Shape shoulders*
Bind off 6 stitches at beginning of next 8 (6, 4, 0) rows, 7 stitches at beginning of next 0 (2, 4, 8) rows. Bind off remaining 31 (33, 35, 35) stitches for back neck.
*Pocket linings* (make 2)
With larger needles and MC, cast on 20 stitches. Work in stockinette stitch for 3½", end with a WS row. Place stitches on hold.

## Right Front
**Note:** Work buttonholes on RS rows as follows: Work 5 stitches, bind off 2 stitches, work to end. On next row, cast on 2 stitches over bound-off stitches.
With larger needles and MC, cast on 51 (55, 59, 63) stitches. Work in seed stitch for 18 rows, AT SAME TIME, work buttonhole on row 9 (9, 9, 11) and cast on 2 stitches at beginning of row 18—53 (57, 61, 65) stitches. Continue in pattern for 14 rows more, working a 2nd buttonhole on 7th (9th, 9th, 11th) row.
*Join pocket lining*
*Next row* (RS) Work 20 stitches, slip next 20 stitches to a holder, then with RS facing, work across 20 stitches of pocket lining, work in pattern to end. Work in pattern for 7 (11, 11, 13) rows more. Continue to work buttonholes and armhole shaping simultaneously as follows: * Work buttonhole on next row, then work 15 (17, 17, 19) rows even; repeat from * twice more, then on next row, work a 6th buttonhole, AT SAME TIME, when piece measures same length as back to underarm, end with a RS

row. Shape armhole at side edge as for back—45 (47, 49, 51) stitches. Work even until armhole measures 7¼ (7¾, 8¼, 8¾)", end with a WS row.
*Shape neck*
*Next row* (RS) Bind off 13 stitches (neck edge), work to end. Decrease 1 stitch at neck edge every row 4 (6, 8, 8) times, then every other row 4 (3, 2, 2) times. Work even until piece measures same length as back to shoulder. Shape shoulder by binding off at beginning of WS rows 6 stitches 4 (3, 2, 0) times, 7 stitches 0 (1, 2, 4) times.

## Left Front
With larger needles and MC, cast on 51 (55, 59, 63) stitches. Work in seed stitch for 16 rows. Cast on 2 stitches at beginning of next row—53 (57, 61, 65) stitches. Work even for 15 rows more.
*Join pocket lining*
*Next row* (RS) Work 13 (17, 21, 25) stitches, slip next 20 stitches to a holder, then with RS facing, work across 20 stitches of pocket lining, work in pattern to end. Work even until piece measures same length as back to underarm, end with a WS row. Shape armhole at side edge as for back—45 (47, 49, 51) stitches. Complete to correspond to right front, working neck shaping at beginning of WS rows and end of RS rows. Shape shoulder by binding off at beginning of RS rows.

## Right Sleeve
*Narrow piece*
With larger needles and MC, cast on 15 stitches. Work in seed stitch for 10 rows. *Next row* (RS) Work to last stitch, increase 1 stitch in next stitch—16 stitches. Work 8 rows even. *Next row* (WS) Work to last stitch, increase 1 stitch in next stitch—17 stitches. Work 8 rows even. *Next row* (RS) Bind off 4 stitches, place remaining 13 stitches on hold. Cut yarn.
*Wide piece*
With larger needles and MC, cast on 37 stitches. Work in seed stitch for 10 rows. *Next row* (RS) Increase 1 stitch in first stitch, work to end—38 stitches. Work 8 rows even. *Next row* (WS) Increase 1 stitch in first stitch, work to end—39 stitches. Work 8 rows even.
*Join pieces*
*Next row* (RS) Work in pattern across 39 stitches of wide piece, then across 13 stitches of narrow piece, increasing 1 stitch at end of row—53 stitches. Work 1 row even. Increase 1 stitch each side (working increases into seed stitch) on next row, then every 16th (12th, 8th, 6th) row 6 (8, 2, 4) times, then every 0 (0, 10th, 8th) row 0 (0, 8, 9) times—67 (71, 75, 81) stitches. Work even until piece measures 16" from beginning, end with a WS row.

*Shape cap*

Bind off 4 stitches at beginning of next 2 rows. Decrease 1 stitch each side on next row, then every 4th row 4 (4, 3, 1) times, then every other row 15 (17, 20, 25) times. Work 1 row even. Bind off remaining 19 stitches.

## Left Sleeve

*Wide piece*

Work as for wide piece of right sleeve, reversing shaping by increasing at end of rows 11 and 20—39 stitches. Do not cut yarn. Place stitches on hold.

*Narrow piece*

Work as for narrow piece of right sleeve for 28 rows, reversing shaping by increasing at beginning of rows 11 and 20—17 stitches. ***Next row*** (RS) Work 13 stitches, increasing 1 stitch at beginning of row, bind off last 4 stitches. Cut yarn. Using same needle, work 39 stitches of wide piece—53 stitches. Complete as for right sleeve.

## Finishing

Block pieces. Sew shoulders.

*Edging*

With RS facing, circular needle and CC, begin at lower right front edge and pick up and knit 47 (52, 52, 53) stitches evenly to top of buttonhole, then pick up and purl 42 (42, 44, 49) stitches along lapel edge and 32 stitches along front neck edge, then pick up and knit 30 (32, 34, 34) stitches along back neck, pick up and purl 32 stitches along left front neck and 42 (42, 44, 49) stitches along lapel edge, pick up and knit 47 (52, 52, 53) stitches along left front edge—272 (284, 290, 302) stitches. ***Rows 1 and 3*** Purl. ***Row 2*** Knit. Bind off knitwise.

*Pockets*

With RS facing, smaller needles and CC, knit 20 stitches from pocket holder. Bind off knitwise. Tack edging to fronts. Sew pocket linings to WS.

Set in sleeves. Sew side seams, leaving 2¼" at lower edges open. Sew sleeve seams.

*Side split edging*

With RS facing, smaller needles and CC, pick up and knit 12 stitches along each side of side split—24 stitches. Bind off knitwise.

*Left sleeve edging*

With RS facing, smaller needles and CC, begin at corner of narrow piece and pick up and knit 50 stitches along lower edge and 16 stitches along side edge of wide piece—66 stitches. Bind off knitwise. Repeat for right sleeve, beginning pickup at top of side edge of wide piece and ending at corner of narrow piece. Sew 2 buttons through both thicknesses on each cuff. Sew buttons on left front. Fold lapels to RS and tack in place or cover with a damp cloth and let dry to keep lapels in place.

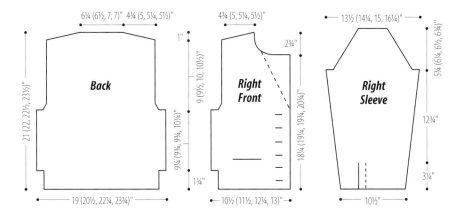

Work or play, this is a jacket for knitters. Simple shaping, great yarn, and fabulous color are only half the fun—the finished fabric looks like giant stockinette stitches!

Kim Dolce

# stockinette cables

### INTERMEDIATE

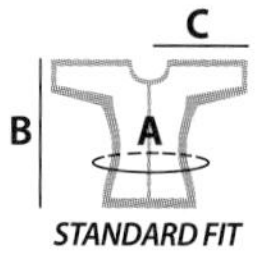

STANDARD FIT

**Sizes** XS (S/M, L, 1X)
**Shown in Small/Medium**
**A** 35½ (40½, 45½, 50)"
**B** 20 (21½, 22¾, 24¼)"
**C** 27 (28½, 30, 31)"

10cm/4"
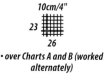
23
26
• **over Charts A and B (worked alternately)**

1 2 3 **4** 5 6

• **Medium weight**
• 1460 (1655, 1875, 2100) yds

• 6.5mm/US 10½,
or size to obtain gauge

• 6.5mm/K-10½

**&**

• stitch marker • stitch holders
• cable needle (cn)

**original yarn**
MANOS DEL URUGUAY Wool (wool;
100g; 138 yds) Henna

## Notes

**1** See *School*, page 94, for SSK, Make 1 (M1), and backward single crochet (sc).
**2** When binding off stitches at top edges of body and sleeves, alternate k1 with k2tog to draw stitches in.

## Back

Cast on 77 (88, 99, 109) stitches. *Row 1* (RS) Knit. *Row 2* Purl. *Row 3* K3, M1, * k2, M1; repeat from *, end k2 (3, 4, 2)—114 (130, 146, 162) stitches. *Row 4* Purl. *Begin Charts A and B: Row 1* (RS) K1, work [8 stitches Chart B] 0 (1, 0, 1) time, [8 stitches Chart A, 8 stitches Chart B] 7 (7, 9, 9) times, [8 stitches Chart A] 0 (1, 0, 1) time, k1. *Row 2* P1, work [8 stitches Chart A] 0 (1, 0, 1) time, [8 stitches Chart B, 8 stitches Chart A] 7 (7, 9, 9) times, [8 stitches Chart B] 0 (1, 0, 1) time, p1. Keeping first and last stitch in stockinette stitch (knit on RS, purl on WS), work charts as established until 8 chart rows have been worked 13 (14, 15, 16) times, then work chart rows 1–6 once more. *Next row* (RS) Bind off all stitches as follows: k1, k2tog, pass first stitch on right needle over 2nd stitch (pfso), * k1, pfso, k2tog, pfso; repeat from *. Piece measures approximately 20 (21½, 22¾, 24¼)" from beginning.

## Right Front

Cast on 39 (44, 50, 56) stitches. *Row 1* (RS) Knit. *Row 2* Purl. *Row 3* K2 (1, 2, 3), M1, * k2, M1; repeat from *, end k1 (1, 2, 3)—58 (66, 74, 82) stitches. *Row 4* Purl. *Begin Charts A and B: Row 1* (RS) K1, work 8 stitches Chart B, [8 stitches Chart A, 8 stitches Chart B] 3 (3, 4, 4) times, [8 stitches Chart A] 0 (1, 0, 1) time, k1. *Row 2* (RS) P1, work [8 stitches Chart A] 0 (1, 0, 1) time, [8 stitches Chart B, 8 stitches Chart A] 3 (3, 4, 4) times, 8 sts Chart B, p1. Continue in chart patterns as established until 8 chart rows have been worked 11 (12, 12, 13) times. *Begin Right Front Neck Shaping Chart (page 12): Row 1* (RS) Work chart for size you are making over first 25 stitches, place marker (pm), work in pattern as established to end. Keeping stitches before marker in Neck Shaping Chart and remaining stitches in pattern as established, work through chart row 2 (2, 6, 6). Piece measures approximately 16¼ (17¾, 18½, 20)" from beginning.

*Shape neck*
Continue in patterns as established, work rows 3–22 (3–22, 7–30, 7–30) of Neck Shaping Chart—42 (49, 55, 61) stitches. Remove marker. Bind off on next row as for back.

## Left Front

Cast on and work 4 rows as for right front. *Begin Charts A and B: Row 1* (RS) K1, work [8 stitches Chart B] 0 (1, 0, 1) time, [8 stitches Chart A, 8 stitches Chart B] 3 (3, 4, 4) times, 8 stitches Chart A, k1. *Row 2* P1, work 8 sts Chart A, [8 stitches Chart B, 8 stitches Chart A] 3 (3, 4, 4) times, [8 stitches Chart B] 0 (1, 0, 1), p1. Complete to correspond to right front, reversing neck shaping by working Left Front Neck Shaping Chart over last 25 stitches.

## Sleeves

**Note:** See Working Increase Stitches on Sleeves, page 11.
Cast on 56 stitches. *Row 1* (RS) Knit. *Row 2* Purl. *Row 3* K1, * k2, M1; repeat from *, end k3—82 stitches. *Row 4* Purl. *Begin Charts A and B: Row 1* (RS) K1, [work 8 stitches Chart A, 8 stitches Chart B] 5 times, k1. Continue in chart patterns as established through Row 8, then work rows 1–6 once more. Increase 1 stitch each side on next row, then every other row 0 (0, 0, 4) times, every 4th row 6 (6, 18, 19) times, every 6th row 10 (10, 2, 0) times—116 (116, 124, 130) stitches. Work even until piece measures 18½" from beginning, end with a WS row. Bind off as for back.

## Finishing

Block pieces. Sew shoulders. Place markers 9 (9, 9½ 10)" down from shoulders on front and back for armholes. Sew top of sleeves between markers. Sew side and sleeve seams.
*Edging*
With RS facing, crochet hook, and 3 strands of yarn held together, begin at side seam and work backward sc along entire outside edge of jacket. Work backward sc around each sleeve cuff.

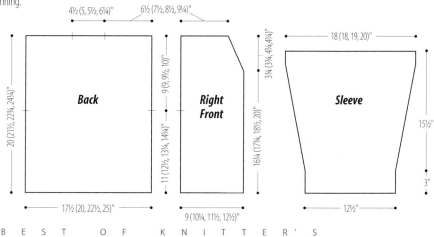

4½ (5, 5½, 6¼)"  6½ (7½, 8½, 9¼)"

20 (21½, 22¾, 24¼)"  **Back**  17½ (20, 22½, 25)"

9 (9, 9½, 10)"

11 (12½, 13¼, 14¼)"  **Right Front**  16¼ (17¾, 18½, 20)"  9 (10¼, 11½, 12½)"

3¾ (3¾, 4½, 4½)"

18 (18, 19, 20)"  **Sleeve**  15½"  3"  12½"

### Chart A

```
8
6         7
4         5
2         3
          1
   8 sts
```

### Chart B

```
8
6         7
4         5
2         3
          1
   8 sts
```

### Stitch key

☐ Knit on RS, purl on WS

⟩⟨ 4/4 RC  Sl 4 to cn, hold to back, k4; k4 from cn

⟩⟨ 4/4 LC  Sl 4 to cn, hold to front, k4; k4 from cn

## TIP:

### WORKING INCREASE STITCHES ON SLEEVES

*1* Keep 1 stitch at each edge in stockinette stitch for selvage.

*2* Work M1 increases inside selvage stitches.

*3* Take stitches into cable pattern as soon as possible by making cable twists of 2 over 1, 2 over 2, 3 over 2, 3 over 3, and 4 over 3, until there are enough stitches for a 4 over 4 cable.

*4* Continue to alternate Charts A and B over additional stitches at each side of sleeve.

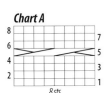

## Neck Shaping Charts

**Right Front (Size XS)**

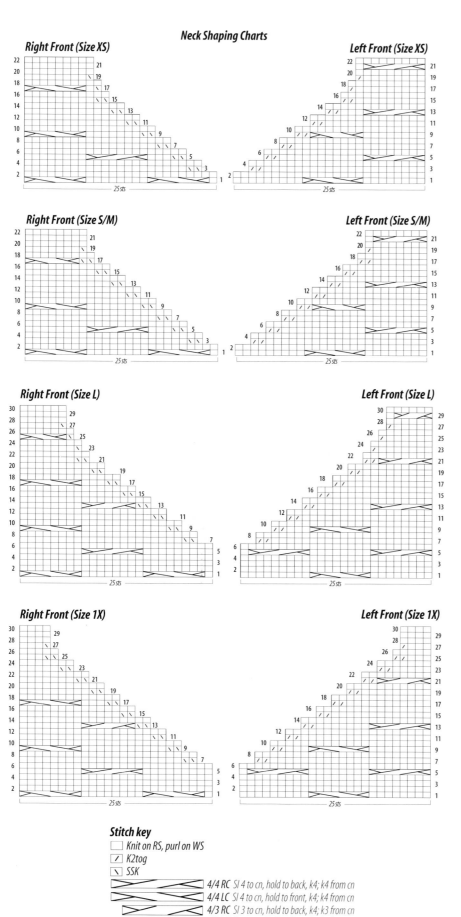

**Left Front (Size XS)**

**Right Front (Size S/M)**

**Left Front (Size S/M)**

**Right Front (Size L)**

**Left Front (Size L)**

**Right Front (Size 1X)**

**Left Front (Size 1X)**

25 sts

### Stitch key

| | |
|---|---|
| ☐ | Knit on RS, purl on WS |
| ✓ | K2tog |
| ✗ | SSK |

| | |
|---|---|
| 4/4 RC | Sl 4 to cn, hold to back, k4; k4 from cn |
| 4/4 LC | Sl 4 to cn, hold to front, k4; k4 from cn |
| 4/3 RC | Sl 3 to cn, hold to back, k4; k3 from cn |
| 4/3 LC | Sl 4 to cn, hold to front, k3; k4 from cn |
| 3/3 LC | Sl 3 to cn, hold to front, k3; k3 from cn |
| 3/2 RC | Sl 2 to cn, hold to back, k3; k2 from cn |

*Precise construction, dressmaker details, and the fabrication are all important elements for the perfect jacket. As a wardrobe basic, you'll wear this jacket for years.*

*Jean Frost*

# resourceful navy

**INTERMEDIATE**

**STANDARD FIT**

**Sizes S (M, L)**
**Shown in Small**
**A** 38 (42¼, 46¼)"
**B** 22½ (23½, 24½)"
**C** 28½ (30½, 32½)"

**10cm/4"**

56
28
• over chart pattern

1 2 **3** 4 5 6

• **Light weight**
**A–C** • 685 (820, 960) yds each

• 3.5mm/US 4,
or size to obtain gauge

• seven 19mm/¾"

• stitch holders
• stitch markers

**original yarn**

BERROCO Harvey (wool; acrylic; polyamid; alpaca; viscose; 50g; 137 yds) Navy (A) Thema (superwash wool; 50g; 132 yds) Teal (B) and Light Olive (C)

## Back

With A, cast on 128 (143, 158) stitches. Knit 1 row on WS. Work in Chart Pattern for 18 (24, 30) rows. Continue in Chart Pattern, decreasing 1 stitch each side on next row, then every 6th row 9 times more—108 (123, 138) stitches. Work 17 (21, 25) rows even. Increase 1 stitch each side (working increases into pattern) on next row, then every 6th row 9 times more—128 (143, 158) stitches. Work even for 43 (47, 45) rows. Piece measures approximately 13½ (14½, 15)" from beginning.
*Shape armholes*
Bind off 7 (9, 10) stitches at beginning of next 2 rows. Decrease 1 stitch each side on next row, then every other row 5 (5, 6) times more—102 (113, 124) stitches. Work even for 107 (107, 111) rows. Armhole measures approximately 8½ (8½, 9)".
*Shape shoulders*
Bind off 10 (11, 12) stitches at beginning of next 2 rows, 11 (12, 13) stitches at beginning of next 4 rows. Bind off remaining 38 (43, 48) stitches.

## Left Front

With A, cast on 71 (80, 86) stitches. Work as for Back, working waist decreases at beginning of RS rows only—61 (70, 76) stitches. Then work waist increases at beginning of RS rows—71 (80, 86) stitches. Work even until piece measures same length as Back to underarm. Shape armhole at beginning of RS rows as for Back—58 (65, 69) stitches. After last decrease row has been worked, work 72 (72, 76) rows even. Armhole measures approximately 6 (6, 6½)".
*Shape neck and shoulder*
**Next row** (WS) Bind off 14 (14, 15) stitches (neck edge), work to end. Decrease 1 stitch at neck edge every row 12 (16, 16) times—32 (35, 38) stitches. Work 22 (18, 18) rows even. Shape shoulder by binding off at beginning of RS rows 10 (11, 12) stitches once, and 11 (12, 13) stitches twice. Place 5 markers for buttons along left front edge, with the first ¾" below neck shaping, the last 5" from lower edge and 3 others spaced evenly between.

## Right Front

Work to correspond to Left Front, reversing all shaping. Work buttonholes to correspond to button markers as follows: At beginning of a RS row, work 4 stitches, bind off next 4 stitches, work to end. On next row, cast on 4 stitches over bound-off stitches.

## Left Sleeve

*Cuff (Narrow Piece)*
With A, cast on 26 (26, 29) stitches. Knit 1 row. Work in Chart Pattern for 36 rows.

**Next row** (RS) Work pattern Row 1 over 21 (21, 24) stitches and place these stitches on hold, bind off remaining stitches. Cut yarn.
*Cuff (Wide Piece)*
With A, cast on 41 (41, 44) stitches. Knit 1 row. Work in Chart Pattern for 12 rows.
**Buttonhole Row** (RS) Work 2 stitches, bind off 4 stitches, work to end. On next row, cast on 4 stitches over bound-off stitches. Continue in pattern until piece measures same as narrow piece, ending with pattern Row 1.
*Join pieces*
**Next row** (WS) Work pattern Row 2 across wide piece, then narrow piece—62 (62, 68) stitches. Continue in pattern as established, AT SAME TIME, increase 1 stitch each side (working increase stitches into pattern) on next row, then every 8th row 19 (22, 10) times, every 10th row 2 (1, 12) times—106 (110, 114) stitches. Work even until piece measures 16 (17, 18)" from beginning, end with a WS row.
*Shape cap*
Bind off 7 (9, 10) stitches at beginning of next 2 rows. Decrease 1 stitch each side on next row, then every other row 18 (18, 19) times more, then every 4th row 9 times. Bind off remaining 36 stitches.

## Right Sleeve

*Cuff (Wide Piece)*
Work as for Left Sleeve, working Buttonhole Row as follows: Work to last 6 stitches, bind off 4 stitches, work to end. When piece is complete, cut yarn and place stitches on hold.
*Cuff (Narrow Piece)*
Work as for Left Sleeve for 36 rows. **Next row** (RS) Bind off 5 stitches, work pattern Row 1 to end.
*Join pieces*
**Next row** (WS) Join pieces by working pattern Row 2 across narrow, then wide piece. Complete to correspond to Left Sleeve.

## Pockets (make 2)

With A, cast on 29 (32, 32) stitches. Knit 1 row. Work 6 rows of Chart Pattern 8 times, then work rows 1-5 once more. Bind off knitwise with A.

## Collar

With A, cast on 119 (122, 125) stitches. Knit 1 row. Work in Chart Pattern for 3", ending with Row 5. Bind off knitwise with A. On each short end of collar, work edging: With RS facing and A, pick up and knit 18 stitches. Knit 1 row. Bind off.

14

## Finishing

Block pieces. Sew shoulders. Begin and end 1" in from each front neck edge, sew collar to neck, with WS of collar facing RS of work.

*Front edgings*

With RS facing and A, begin at lower edge of Right Front and pick up and knit 110 (115, 120) stitches to neck edge, then 5 stitches across top of neck to collar. Knit 1 row. Bind off. Work Left Front as for Right Front, beginning pick-up row at collar.

*Cuffs*

With RS facing and A, pick up and knit 12 stitches along side edge of wide piece nearest buttonhole. Work edging as before. Center pockets on fronts about 1" from lower edge and sew in place. Set in sleeves. Tack bound-off stitches of cuff to WS. Sew side and sleeve seams. Sew buttons on Left Front and on narrow piece of Sleeve cuffs.

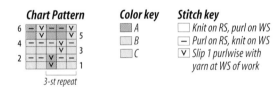

**Chart Pattern**

**Color key**
- A
- B
- C

**Stitch key**
- Knit on RS, purl on WS
- Purl on RS, knit on WS
- V Slip 1 purlwise with yarn at WS of work

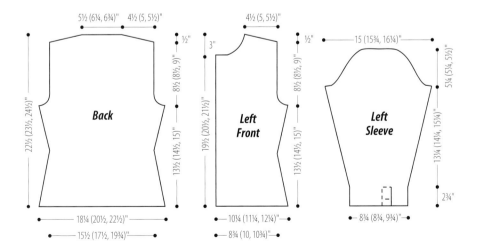

Kathy Zimmerman

*This classically-styled jacket can be dressed up or down depending on your needs. For faster knitting and a tweed look, Kathy has combined a strand each of two lighter-weight yarns. The matching plum yarn trim and dyed-to-match buttons make this a truly coordinated effort.*

# a well-bred plum

**INTERMEDIATE**

**STANDARD FIT**

**Sizes S (M, L, 1X, 2X)**
**Shown in Small**
A 39¾ (43, 45½, 48¾, 52½)"
B 22 (23, 23½, 24, 25)"
C 28 (29, 30, 31, 31½)"

**10cm/4"**
27
15
• over seed stitch,
using larger needles and A and B
held together

1 2 **3** 4 5 6
• **Light weight**
• A & B 1080 (1200, 1300, 1400, 1510) yds each

1 2 3 **4** 5 6
• **Medium weight**
• C 150 (160, 170, 180, 190) yds

• 5mm/US 8 and 5.5mm/US 9, or
size to obtain gauge, 74cm/29" long

• 9 (9, 9, 10, 10) 23mm/⅞"

**&**
• stitch holders
• stitch markers

**original yarn**

BERROCO Europa (wool blend; 50g; 135 yds) Berry (A); LANG Ronda (wool blend; 50g; 143 yds) Plum (B); BERROCO Sensu Wool (wool blend; 50g; 96 yds) Plum (C)

## Notes

**1** See *School*, page 94, for SSK, SSP and 3-needle bind-off. **2** Work body in one piece to underarm, then divide for fronts and back. **3** Jacket is worked with 1 strand each of A and B held together, or use 1 strand of a medium-weight yarn. Work edgings with 1 strand of C. **4** Measure pieces with edges rolled. **5** For ease in working, mark RS of work.

## Seed stitch

*Row 1* * K1, p1; repeat from *.
*Row 2* Knit the purl stitches and purl the knit stitches. Repeat row 2 for seed stitch.

## Pocket linings (make 2)

With larger needle and 1 strand each of A and B, cast on 19 stitches. Work in seed stitch for 4¼". Place stitches on hold.

## Decrease rows

*At beginning of RS rows* K1, SSK.
*At end of RS rows* K2tog, k1.
*At beginning of WS rows* P1, p2tog.
*At end of WS rows* SSP, p1.

## Body

With smaller needle and 1 strand C, cast on 145 (157, 167, 179, 193) stitches. Beginning with a purl row, work in stockinette stitch (St st; knit on RS rows, purl on WS rows) for 8 rows. Change to larger needle and 1 strand each A and B. Purl 1 row. Work in seed stitch until piece measures 4½" from beginning, end with a WS row.
*Pocket buttonhole row* (RS) Work 15 (17, 19, 21, 23) stitches, yarn over (yo), k2tog, work to last 17 (19, 21, 23, 25) stitches of row, SSK, yo, work to end. Work 3 rows even.
*Place pocket*
*Next row* (RS) Work 6 (8, 10, 12, 14) stitches, * place next 19 stitches on hold, then with RS of pocket lining facing, work across 19 stitches of pocket lining *, work to last 25 (27, 29, 31, 33) stitches of row, repeat between *'s once, work to end. Work even until piece measures 13½ (14, 14, 14, 15)" from beginning, end with a WS row.
*Divide for fronts and back*
*Next row* (RS) Work 27 (30, 32, 34, 37) stitches (right front), bind off 17 (17, 18, 20, 21)

stitches (underarm), work until there are 57 (63, 67, 71, 77) stitches for back, bind off 17 (17, 18, 20, 21) stitches (underarm), work to end (left front). *Next row* (WS) Work 27 (30, 32, 34, 37) stitches of left front. Place all other stitches on hold.

## Left Front

Work even until armhole measures 4½ (5, 5, 5½, 5½)", end with a WS row.
*Shape neck*
*Next row* (RS) Work to last 3 stitches (neck edge), k2tog, k1. Continue to decrease 1 stitch at neck edge every row 0 (2, 0, 2, 4) times, then every other row 9 (8, 11, 10, 9) times—17 (19, 20, 21, 23) stitches. Work even until armhole measures 8½ (9, 9½, 10, 10)". Place stitches on hold.

## Right Front

With WS facing, join yarn at underarm and work to correspond to left front. Reverse neck shaping by working decreases at beginning of RS rows and end of WS rows.

## Back

With WS facing, join yarn at underarm and work even until armhole measures 7½ (8, 8½, 9, 9)", end with a WS row.
*Shape neck*
*Next row* (RS) Work 20 (22, 23, 24, 26) stitches, join 2nd ball of yarn and bind off center 17 (19, 21, 23, 25) stitches, work to end. Working both sides at same time, decrease 1 stitch at each neck edge every row 3 times—17 (19, 20, 21, 23) stitches each side. Work even until armhole measures same length as fronts to shoulder. Place stitches on hold.

## Sleeves

**Note:** Work increases one stitch in from edge.
With smaller needle and 1 strand C, cast on 33 (35, 37, 37, 39) stitches. Beginning with a purl row, work in stockinette stitch for 8 rows. Change to larger needle and 1 strand each A and B. Purl 1 row. Work in seed stitch, AT SAME TIME, increase 1 stitch each side (working increases into pattern) on 5th row, then every 6th row 2 (2, 6, 14, 10) times, then every 8th row 13 (13, 10, 4, 7) times—65 (67, 71, 75, 75) stitches. Piece measures approximately 18½" from beginning. Work even for 2¼ (2¼, 2½, 2¾, 2¾)". Bind off.

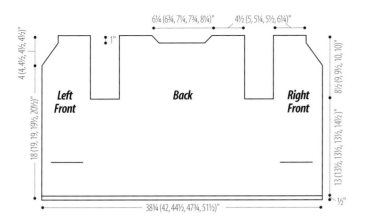

Left Front · Back · Right Front

Sleeve

4 (4, 4½, 4½, 4½)"

18 (19, 19, 19½, 20½)"

1"

6¼ (6¾, 7¼, 7¾, 8¼)"    4½ (5, 5¼, 5½, 6¼)"

8½ (9, 9½, 10, 10)"

13 (13½, 13½, 13½, 14½)"

½"

38¾ (42, 44½, 47¾, 51½)"

17 (18, 19, 20, 20)"

2¼ (2¼, 2½, 2¾, 2¾)"

18"

½"

8¾ (9½, 10, 10, 10½)"

## Finishing

Block pieces. Join shoulders, using 3-needle bind-off.

*Neckband*

With RS facing, smaller needle, and 1 strand C, pick up and knit 87 (91, 95, 99, 103) stitches evenly around neck edge. Beginning with a purl row, work in St st for 1½". Bind off loosely.

*Buttonband*

With RS facing, smaller needle, and 1 strand C, begin just below neck-band and pick up and knit 85 (89, 89, 91, 95) stitches evenly along left front edge, ending just above rolled edge. Work in k1, p1 rib for 1". Bind off in rib. Place 7 (7, 7, 8, 8) markers along band for buttons, with the first ¾" below neck edge, the last 1½" from lower edge and 5 (5, 5, 6, 6) others spaced evenly between.

*Buttonhole band*

Work as for buttonband, working buttonholes (yo, work 2 together) opposite markers when band measures ½".

*Pocket bands*

With RS facing, smaller needle, and 1 strand C, knit across 19 pocket stitches on hold. Work 7 rows more in St st. Bind off loosely.

Sew top of sleeves to straight edges of armholes. Sew straight portion at top of sleeves to bound-off underarm stitches. Sew sleeve seams. Sew buttons on buttonband and on each pocket lining to correspond to buttonholes. Tack sides of rolled edges at pockets, front neck, and lower front edges.

*Swatch shown with one strand of ROWAN Scottish Tweed 4ply Aran (wool; 100g; 187 yds) instead of A/B held together.*

# HOW TO

## PICK UP AND KNIT VERTICALLY (AND DIAGONALLY)

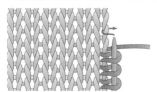 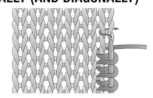

Insert needle 2 sizes smaller than garment needles *into* center of first stitch, catch yarn and knit a stitch.

For an even firmer edge, insert needle in space *between* first and 2nd stitches.

## HORIZONTALLY

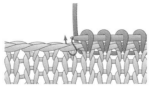

Along a horizontal edge, insert needle into center of the stitch.

## VERTICAL AND DIAGONAL PICK-UP RATE

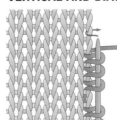

*Example shows picking up 3 stitches for every 4 rows of stockinette stitch.*

### TIP

*The ratio of picked-up stitches to rows is based on the pattern's row gauge. It is wise to test the formula by picking up stitches on your gauge swatch, working the border, and binding off.*

Jean Frost

*Using a textured yarn as a base, Jean created an easy-to-knit style that's elegant to wear. Instead of going to great lengths to create a jacket fabric, the yarn does the work. The crocheted trim and coordinating buttons complete this refined look.*

# revisited Chanel

**INTERMEDIATE**

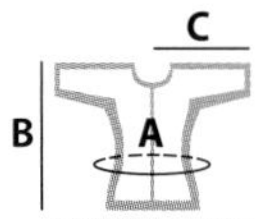

**STANDARD FIT**

**Sizes S (M, L, 1X)**
**Shown in Medium**
**A** 40¾ (44¾, 48¾, 51¾)"
**B** 21¾ (23¼, 24¼, 24¾)"
**C** 29 (31, 33½, 34½)"

**10cm/4"**
**24**
**12**
• over reverse stockinette stitch (purl on RS, knit on WS), using MC

1 2 3 4 **5** 6
• **Bulky weight**
**MC** • 460 (525, 610, 640) yds

1 2 3 **4** 5 6
• **Medium weight**
**CC** • 130 (140, 150, 160) yds

5mm/US 8,
or size to obtain gauge

4mm/G-6

• five 20mm/¾"
• eight 15mm/⅝"

• stitch holders
• stitch markers

**original yarn**
STACY CHARLES/FILATURA DI CROSA Sapporo (mohair blend; 50g; 44 yds) in Fuchsia Tweed (MC); Primo (wool; 50g; 76 yds) in burgundy or gold (CC)

## Notes
**1** See *School*, page 94, for SSP, 3-needle bind-off, half-double crochet (hdc), and chain stitch. **2** For ease in working, mark RS of work.

## Back
With MC, cast on 60 (66, 72, 75) stitches. Work in reverse stockinette stitch (rev St st) for 13 (14, 14½, 14½)", end with a WS row.
*Shape armholes*
Bind off 4 (5, 6, 6) stitches at beginning of next 2 rows. Decrease 1 stitch each side every row 4 times—44 (48, 52, 55) stitches. Work even until armhole measures 8 (8½, 9, 9½)", end with a WS row. Place stitches on hold.

## Right Front
With MC, cast on 30 (33, 36, 39) stitches. Work in rev St st until piece measures same length as back to underarm, end with a WS row.
*Shape V-neck and armhole*
*Next row* (RS) P1, p2tog, purl to end. Shape armhole at side edge as for back, AT SAME TIME, continue to decrease 1 stitch at neck edge (beginning of RS rows) every 4th row 6 (7, 9, 13) times, every 6th row 3 (3, 2, 0) times—12 (13, 14, 15) stitches. Work even until armhole measures same length as back to shoulder, end with a WS row. Place stitches on hold.

## Left Front
Work as for right front, reversing shaping. For V-neck, work SSP, p1 at end of RS rows.

## Right Sleeve
*Work placket*
With MC, cast on 16 (16, 17, 17) stitches, then with 2nd ball of yarn, cast on 14 (14, 15, 15) stitches onto same needle. Working both pieces at same time, work in rev St st for 3", end with a WS row. *Next row* (RS) P1, increase 1 stitch in next stitch, purl to end of first piece; purl to last 2 stitches of 2nd piece, increase 1 stitch in next stitch, p1. Continue to increase 1 stitch at each side every 14th (10th, 10th, 10th) row 2 (7, 6, 6) times, then every 12th (0, 8th, 8th) row 3 (0, 2, 2) times (join pieces when work measures 6" from beginning by working across all stitches with first ball of yarn, breaking 2nd ball of yarn)—42 (46, 50, 50) stitches. Work even until piece measures 15 (16, 17, 17)" from beginning, end with a WS row.

*Shape cap*
Bind off 4 (5, 6, 6) stitches at beginning of next 2 rows. Decrease 1 stitch each side on next row, then every 4th row 7 (7, 8, 9) times more, every other row 0 (1, 1, 0) time, every row 3 times. Bind off 3 stitches at beginning of next 2 rows. Bind off remaining 6 stitches.

## Left Sleeve
*Work placket*
With MC, cast on 14 (14, 15, 15) stitches, then with 2nd ball of yarn, cast on 16 (16, 17, 17) stitches onto same needle. Complete as for right sleeve.

## Pockets (make 2)
With MC, cast on 18 stitches. Work in rev St st for 4½". Bind off.

## Finishing
Block pieces. Join shoulders, using 3-needle bind-off, as follows: Join 12 (13, 14, 15) stitches of first shoulder, then bind off back neck stitches until 12 (13, 14, 15) stitches remain, join 2nd shoulder. Set in sleeves. Sew side and sleeve seams.

## Crocheted Bands
**Notes: 1** Work all bands with RS facing, crochet hook and CC. **2** On all rows, work 4 hdc in lower-edge corner stitch of right and left fronts, and 3 hdc at first V-neck decrease row.
*Body front and back band*
Place 5 markers for buttonholes along right front edge, the first just below first V-neck decrease, the last ½" above lower edge, and 3 others spaced evenly between. *Begin crocheted band: Row 1* Begin at right side seam and work hdc evenly around entire jacket edge. Do not turn. *Row 2* Work hdc around, working into both legs of stitches. *Row 3* Repeat row 2, working a buttonhole (chain 2, skip 2 stitches) at each buttonhole marker on right front. *Row 4* Work hdc around. Fasten off.
*Right sleeve band*
**Note:** Work 4 hdc in lower-edge corner stitch of wider piece on all rows.
Place 3 markers for buttonholes along edge of wider piece, with the first ¾" below top of placket, the last ½" above lower edge, and 1 centered between. *Begin crocheted band: Row 1* Join yarn at top of placket and work hdc along edge of placket, around lower edge of sleeve to corner of narrower piece. Cut yarn. *Rows 2 and 4* Rejoin yarn to beginning of row and work hdc. Cut yarn. *Row 3* Repeat row 2, working buttonholes as before at markers.

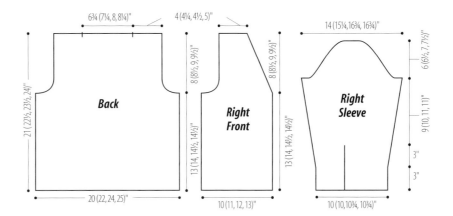

6¾ (7¼, 8, 8¼)"    4 (4¼, 4½, 5)"    14 (15¼,16¾, 16¾)"

**Back**

**Right Front**

**Right Sleeve**

21 (22½, 23½, 24)"

8 (8½, 9, 9½)"    8 (8½, 9, 9½)"

6 (6½, 7, 7½)"

13 (14, 14½)"    13 (14, 14½)"

9 (10, 11, 11)"

3"

3"

20 (22, 24, 25)"    10 (11, 12, 13)"    10 (10,10¾, 10¾)"

*Left sleeve band*

Work as for right sleeve band, beginning at corner of narrow piece and working along lower edge of sleeve and along placket edge of wide piece.

*Pocket band*

Work bands along top of each pocket as for sleeves, omitting buttonholes.

Using photo as guide, center pockets on fronts and sew approximately 1" above lower-edge band. Sew 5 larger buttons on left front band opposite buttonholes. Sew 1 smaller button centered on each pocket band. Sew 3 smaller buttons on each sleeve opposite buttonholes.

Swatch shows reverse stockinette stitch with half-double crochet edge.
CLAUDIA HAND PAINTED YARNS Boucle (kid mohair, wool, nylon; 200g; 432 yds) navy/olive (MC) and CLAUDIA HAND PAINTED YARNS Chunky weight (wool; 100g; 103 yds) navy/olive

*Rich hues of kid mohair yarn in a tweedy blend help to create a jacket suitable for many work environ-ments. Linen stitch on an unexpectedly large needle—size 10½ (6.5 mm), makes a great suiting fabric. The elegant mahogany-colored accents and trim fit make this jacket the perfect wear-to-work separate.*

# workplace mahogany

**INTERMEDIATE**

**STANDARD FIT**

**Sizes S (M, L, 1X)**
**Shown in Medium**
**A** 38 (41, 46, 48½)"
**B** 22 (22½, 23, 23½)"
**C** 29 (30½, 31, 32½)"

10cm/4"
32
20
• over linen stitch,
using 6.5mm/US 10½ needles

1 2 3 **4** 5 6

• Medium weight
**A** • 530 (595, 660, 700) yds
**B–G** • 175 (200, 215, 235) yds of each

• 5mm/US 8, 5.5mm/US 9,
and 6.5mm/US 10½,
*or size to obtain gauge*

• seven 13mm/½"

• 3.25mm/D-3

**&**
• stitch holders
• stitch markers

*original yarn*

## Note
See *School*, page 94, for SSP, SK2P and single crochet.

## Linen Stitch (over an even number of sts)
*Row 1* (RS) * K1, with yarn in front, slip 1 (sl 1) purlwise; repeat from * to last 2 stitches, k2. *Row 2* * P1, with yarn in back, sl 1 purlwise; repeat from * to last 2 stitches, p2. Repeat Rows 1 and 2 for linen stitch.

## Stripe Pattern
Work 1 row each in the following color sequence: * B, C, A, D, E, A, F, G, A; repeat from * (9 rows) for Stripe Pattern.

## Back
With size 6.5mm/US10½ needles and A, cast on 96 (104, 116, 122) stitches. Work in linen stitch and Stripe Pattern, AT SAME TIME, decrease 1 stitch each side on 9th row, then every 8th row 5 times more—84 (92, 104, 110) stitches. Work even until piece measures 7½" from beginning, end with a WS row. Increase 1 stitch each side on next row, then every 10th row 3 times more—92 (100, 112, 118) stitches. Work even until piece measures 13" from beginning, end with a WS row.
*Shape armholes*
Bind off 5 (5, 6, 6) stitches at beginning of next 2 rows, 2 stitches at beginning of next 2 (4, 6, 6) rows. Decrease 1 stitch each side every RS row 3 (3, 4, 5) times—72 (76, 80, 84) stitches. Work even until armhole measures 8 (8½, 9, 9½)", end with a WS row. Mark center 14 (18, 18, 22) stitches.
*Shape shoulders and neck*
Bind off 5 stitches at beginning of next 4 rows, 5 (5, 6, 6) stitches at beginning of next 4 rows, AT SAME TIME, join 2nd ball of yarn and bind off stitches between markers and, working both sides at same time, bind off from each neck edge 3 stitches 3 times.

## Left Front
With size 6.5mm/US 10½ needles and A, cast on 48 (52, 58, 62) stitches. Work in linen stitch and Stripe Pattern, working decreases at beginning of RS rows as for back—42 (46, 52, 56) stitches. Work even until piece measures 7½" from beginning, end with a WS row. Work increases at beginning of RS rows as for back—46 (50, 56, 60) stitches. Work even until piece measures same length as

back to underarm, end with a WS row. Shape armhole at beginning of RS rows as for back—36 (38, 40, 43) stitches. Work even until armhole measures 6½ (7, 7½, 8)", end with a RS row.
*Shape neck*
*Next row* (WS) Bind off 5 (6, 6, 6) stitches, work to end. * *Next row* (RS) Work to last 3 stitches, k3tog. *Next row* P2tog, work to end. Repeat from * 2 (2, 2, 3) times more. ** Work 1 row even. *Next row* (WS) P2tog, work to end. Repeat from ** 1 (2, 2, 2) times more, AT SAME TIME, when armhole measures same length as back to shoulder, shape shoulder at beginning of RS rows as for back.

## Right Front
Work as for left front, reversing shaping. Work waist decreases and increases at end of RS rows. Shape armhole at beginning of WS rows and end of RS rows.
*Shape neck*
*Next row* (RS) Bind off 5 (6, 6, 6) stitches, work to end. Work 1 row even. * *Next row* (RS) SK2P, work to end. *Next row* Work to last 2 stitches, SSP. Repeat from * 2 (2, 2, 3) times more. ** Work 1 row even. *Next row* (WS) Work to last 2 stitches, SSP. Repeat from ** 1 (2, 2, 2) times more, AT SAME TIME, when armhole measures same length as back to shoulder, shape shoulder at beginning of WS rows as for back.

## Sleeves
With size 6.5mm/US 10½ needles and A, cast on 50 (52, 54, 58) stitches. Work in linen stitch for 2½", end with a WS row. Continue in linen stitch and work in Stripe Pattern, AT SAME TIME, increase 1 stitch each side (working increases into pattern) on 7th row, then every 6th row 3 (1, 9, 7) times, every 8th row 10 (12, 6, 8) times—78 (80, 86, 90) stitches. Work even until piece measures 16½ (17, 17, 17½)" from beginning, end with a WS row.
*Shape cap*
Bind off 5 (5, 6, 6) stitches at beginning of next 2 rows, 2 stitches at beginning of next 6 (8, 10, 10) rows. Decrease 1 stitch each side on next row, then every other row 12 (16, 14, 16) times more. Work 1 row even. Bind off 2 stitches at beginning of next 10 (4, 6, 6) rows. Bind off remaining 10 (10, 12, 12) stitches.

## Collar
With size 5.5mm/US 9 needles and A, cast on 86 (94, 94, 98) stitches. Work in linen stitch for 2¾", end with a WS row. Bind off loosely knitwise.

## Pockets (make 2)
With size 6.5mm/US 10½ needles and G, cast on 26 stitches. Change to A and work 1 row of linen stitch pattern. Then continue in linen stitch and Stripe Pattern

CYNTHIA HELENE Kid Mohair (mohair blend; 50g; 99 yds) Red Mahogany (A), Blush (B), Smokey Green (C), Khaki (D), Russet (E), Chamois (F), Mink (G)

(beginning with B) until piece measures 3¼" from beginning, end with a WS row. Change to size 5.5mm/US 9 needles and A. Work linen stitch for ¾", end with a WS row. Bind off knitwise. With RS facing, crochet hook, and A, work 1 row single crochet (sc) through back loops of bind-off row.

## Finishing

Block pieces.

## Buttonband

With RS facing, size 5mm/US 8 needles, and A, pick up and knit 108 (110, 112, 114) stitches evenly along left front edge. Work in linen stitch for 1" beginning with a WS row. Bind off loosely. Work crocheted edging (as for pockets) across top of band at neck edge and along left front, working 2 sc in each corner. Sew 7 buttons on band, with the first and last ½" from neck and lower edge and 5 others spaced evenly between.

## Buttonhole band

Work to correspond to buttonband, working buttonholes opposite buttons on Row 4 by binding off 2 stitches for each buttonhole, then on next row, casting on 2 stitches over bound-off stitches. Work crocheted edging along band, then across top of neck edge. Sew pockets to fronts, matching colors of Stripe Pattern, with each pocket 4" in from edge of front band, and ¾" above lower edge. Sew shoulders. Sew cast-on edge of collar around neck edge, easing to fit. Work crocheted edging around collar. Set in sleeves. Sew side and sleeve seams.

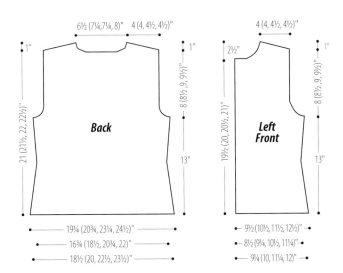

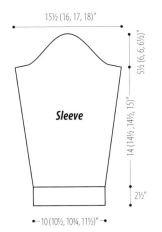

Katharine Hunt

# metro jacket

*City sophisticates will love this clean, crisp jacket that features a textured slip-stitch fabric. Tailored accents and a zip front make it a perfect coordinate piece for many occasions.*

**INTERMEDIATE +**

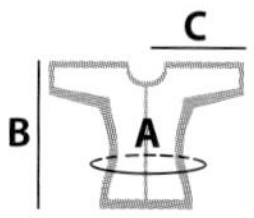

**STANDARD FIT**

**XS (S, M, L, 1X)**
**Shown in Medium**
**A** 33½ (37½, 40½, 44½, 48½)"
**B** 21¾ (22¾, 23¾, 24¾, 25¾)"
**C** 28 (29, 29½, 30, 31)"

**10cm/4"**

42
24
• over chart pattern

1 2 **3** 4 5 6

• **Light weight**
A • 780 (870, 940, 1040, 1140) yds

1 2 3 **4** 5 6

• **Medium weight**
B • 900 (1000, 1080, 1200, 1315) yds

• 3.75mm/US 5
or size to obtain gauge

• stitch markers
• zipper
• decorative tassel (optional)

**original yarn**
SR KERTZER Denim Freedom DK
(cotton; 50g; 103 yds) Natural (A)
SR KERTZER Beaux (cotton blend;
50g; 103 yds) Taupe (B)

## Notes

**1** See *School*, page 94, for long-tail cast-on, stranded 2-color knitting, Make 1 (M1), and zippers. **2** Use long-tail cast-on throughout. **3** When working shaping, omit slip (sl) stitches if they fall at the edge. **4** When working 3-stitch garter borders, twist yarns together at point where color A of border meets color B of main pattern by bringing new yarn under old yarn.

## Back

With A, cast on 99 (111, 123, 135, 147) stitches. Knit 4 rows. *Begin Chart Pattern: Row 1* (RS) K3A, join B and work first 3 stitches of chart, then work 6-stitch repeat across to last 3 stitches, join 2nd ball of A and k3. Continue in Chart Pattern as established, keeping 3 stitches at each side in garter stitch with A, until 12 rows of chart have been worked twice. Cut 2nd ball of A. *Next row* (RS) Work chart row 7 over all stitches (discontinue 3-stitch garter border each side). Work chart rows 8–12, then work rows 1–4 once.
*Shape waist*
Continue in Chart Pattern as established, decrease 1 stitch each side on next row, then every 18th (18th, 12th, 12th, 12th) row 2 (2, 4, 4, 4) times more—93 (105, 113, 125, 137) stitches. Work 23 (29, 23, 29, 35) rows even. Increase 1 stitch each side on next row, then every 18th (18th, 12th, 12th, 12th) row 2 (2, 3, 3, 3) times more—99 (111, 121, 133, 145) stitches. Work 5 (5, 3, 3, 3) rows even. Piece measures approximately 13½ (14, 14½, 15, 15½)" from beginning.
*Shape armholes*
Bind off 4 (6, 10, 13, 15) stitches at beginning of next 2 rows. Decrease 1 stitch each side on next row, then every other row 1 (1, 2, 3, 4) times more—87 (95, 95, 99, 105) stitches. Work even until armhole measures 7½ (8, 8½, 9, 9½)", end with a WS row.
*Shape shoulders and neck*
Bind off 6 (6, 6, 6, 7) stitches at beginning of next 6 rows, then 5 (7, 7, 8, 7) stitches at beginning of next 2 rows, AT SAME TIME, join 2nd ball of yarn and bind off center 31 (35, 35, 37, 39) stitches for neck and, working both sides at same time, decrease 1 stitch at each neck edge every row 5 times.

## Left Front

With A, cast on 51 (57, 63, 69, 75) stitches. Work as for back until 12 rows of chart have been worked twice above garter border. Do not cut 2nd ball of A. *Next row* (RS) Work chart row 7 to last 3 stitches of row, with A, k3. Continue in pattern, working waist shaping at side edge only as for back and keeping 3 stitches at front edge in garter stitch with A—48 (54, 58, 64, 70) stitches after decreases, then 51 (57, 62, 68, 74) stitches after increases. When piece measures same length as back to underarm, shape armhole at side edge as for back—45 (49, 49, 51, 54) stitches. Work even until armhole measures 5¼ (5¾, 6¼, 6, 6½)", end with a RS row.

*Shape neck*
**Next row** (WS) Bind off 10 (12, 12, 12, 12) stitches (neck edge), work to end. Decrease 1 stitch at neck edge every row 5 (5, 5, 3, 5) times, then every other row 7 (7, 7, 10, 9) times—23 (25, 25, 26, 28) stitches. Work even until armhole measures same length as back to shoulder. Shape shoulder at beginning of RS rows as for back.

## Right Front

Work as for left front until 12 rows of chart have been worked twice above garter border. Cut 2nd ball of A. **Next row** (RS) K3A, then work chart row 1, ending with 3rd stitch of repeat. Complete to correspond to left front, reversing shaping.

## Left Sleeve

With A, cast on 44 (45, 45, 47, 48) stitches, then with a 2nd ball of A, cast on 13 (14, 14, 16, 17) stitches. Working both sections at the same time, knit 4 rows. Join B and work chart pattern as follows: *Row 1* (RS) *First section*: K1 (2, 2, 4, 5), sl 1, k5, sl 1, k2, join 3rd ball of A and k3; *2nd section*: With A, k3, join B and k3, [sl 1, k5] 6 times, sl 1, k1 (2, 2, 4, 5). Work 3 rows in pattern as established, keeping 3 stitches at each side of sleeve vent in garter stitch with A. **Next row** (RS) With A, k1, M1, knit to end of first section; on 2nd section, with A, knit to last stitch, M1, k1. Work 1 row even in pattern. **Next row** (RS) With B, k5 (6, 6, 2, 3), [sl 1, k5] 1 (1, 1, 2, 2) times, k3A; k3A, then with B, k6, [sl 1, k5] 5 (5, 5, 6, 6) times, sl 1, k5 (6, 6, 2, 3). Continue in pattern as established for 13 rows more, AT SAME TIME, increase 1 stitch each side (working increases into chart pattern) on 4th and 10th row—16 (17, 17, 19, 20) stitches in first section; 47 (48, 48, 50, 51) stitches in 2nd section.
*Join sections*
**Next row** (RS) Work Chart Pattern to last 3 stitches of first section, k3A, then with same ball of A, knit first 3 stitches of 2nd section (cut other ball of A), then work in Chart Pattern to end. **Next row** Work Chart Pattern over 44 (45, 45, 47, 48) stitches, k6A, work Chart Pattern to end. **Next row** (RS) With A, k1, M1, knit to last stitch (cut 2nd ball of A and B), M1, k1. **Next row** P45 (46, 46, 48, 49), k6, p14 (15, 15, 17, 18). **Next row** (RS) Work Chart Pattern as established over all stitches. Continue in Chart Pattern, increasing 1 stitch each side every 12th (10th, 8th, 8th, 6th) row 4 (6, 6, 13, 2) times, then every 14th (12th, 10th, 10th, 8th) row 9 (9, 12, 6, 19) times—91 (97, 103, 109, 115) stitches. Piece measures approximately—19½ (19, 19, 18½, 18½)" from beginning.
*Shape cap*
Work 7 (11, 19, 23, 27) rows even. Decrease 1 stitch each side every row 4 (4, 6, 8, 8) times. Bind off remaining 83 (89, 91, 93, 99) stitches.

## Right Sleeve

With A, cast on 13 (14, 14, 16, 17) stitches, then with a 2nd ball of A, cast on 44 (45, 45, 47, 48) stitches. Working both sections at the same time, knit 4 rows. Join B and work

### Chart pattern

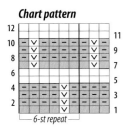

6-st repeat

### Stitch key

☐ Knit on RS, purl on WS

☐ Purl on RS, knit on WS

☑ Sl 1 purlwise with yarn at WS of work

### Color key

☐ A

☐ B

Chart Pattern as follows: **Row 1** (RS) *First Section:* K1 (2, 2, 4, 5), [sl 1, k5] 6 times, sl 1, k3, join 3rd ball of A and k3; *2nd Section:* With A, k3, join B and k2, sl 1, k5, sl 1, k1 (2, 2, 4, 5). Work 3 rows in pattern as established, keeping 3 stitches at each side of sleeve vent in garter stitch with A. **Next row** (RS) With A, k1, M1, knit to end of first section; on 2nd section, with A, knit to last stitch, M1, k1. Work 1 row even in pattern. **Next row** (RS) With B, k5 (6, 6, 2, 3), [sl 1, k5] 5 (5, 5, 6, 6) times, sl 1, k6, k3A; k3A, then with B, k5, [sl 1, k5] 0 (0, 0, 1, 1) time, sl 1, k5 (6, 6, 2, 3). Continue in pattern as established for 13 rows more, AT SAME TIME, increase 1 stitch each side (working increases into Chart Pattern) on 4th and 10th row—47 (48, 48, 50, 51) stitches in first section; 16 (17, 17, 19, 20) stitches in 2nd section.

*Join sections*

**Next row** (RS) Work Chart Pattern to last 3 stitches of first section, k3A, then with same ball of A, knit first 3 stitches of 2nd section (cut other ball of A), then work in Chart Pattern to end. **Next row** Work Chart Pattern over 13 (14, 14, 16, 17) stitches, k6A, work Chart Pattern to end. **Next row** (RS) With A, k1, M1, knit to last stitch (cut 2nd ball of A and B), M1, k1. **Next row** P14 (15, 15, 17, 18), k6, p45 (46, 46, 48, 49). **Next row** (RS) Work Chart Pattern as established over all stitches. Complete as for left sleeve.

### Finishing

Block pieces. Sew shoulders.

*Neckband*

With RS facing and A, begin at right front edge and pick up and knit 110 (118, 118, 128, 134) stitches evenly around neck edge. Knit 3 rows. **Next row** (RS) Knit, decreasing 4 stitches evenly across back neck and 1 stitch in center of each front neck curve—104 (112, 112, 122, 128) stitches. Bind off knitwise on WS.

Insert zipper, lining up bottom of zipper with top of side vents. Set in sleeves, with vents at back. Sew side and sleeve seams. Attach tassel to zipper tab (optional).

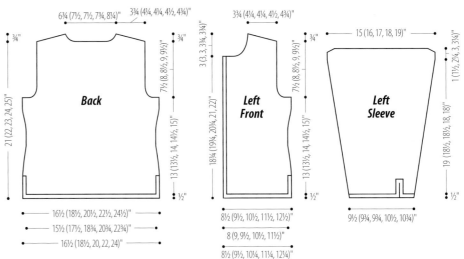

*This is a "suit-able" jacket that will move easily from workdays to evenings to casual Saturdays. Norah created her fitted garment using vertical openwork and cables. The vertical lines work neatly into the cabled yoke design. Her yarn choice: a fluid alpaca in an autumny tone.*

# uptown toffee

**INTERMEDIATE**

**STANDARD FIT**

**Sizes S (M, L)**
**Shown in Medium**
**A** 36¾ (40¾, 44¾)"
**B** 21½ (23, 24½)"
**C** 27 (29, 31)"

**10cm/4"**

32
20/25

• over Chart A
• over Chart G, fully extended (wet blocking recommended)

1 2 3 **4** 5 6

• **Medium weight**
1150 (1380, 1595) yds

4mm/US 6,
*or size to obtain gauge*

• six 20mm/¾"

**&**
• stitch markers
• cable needle (cn)

***original yarn***
CLASSIC ELITE YARNS
Inca Alpaca (alpaca;
50g; 115 yds) Toffee

## Back

Cast on 122 (134, 146) stitches. *Begin chart patterns: Row 1* (RS) Work 2 (8, 10) stitches Chart A, 18 stitches Chart B, 0 (0, 4) stitches Chart C, 28 stitches Chart D, 26 stitches Chart E, 28 stitches Chart D, 0 (0, 4) stitches Chart A, 18 stitches Chart B, 2 (8, 10) stitches Chart C. *Row 2* Work 2 (8, 10) stitches Chart C, 18 stitches Chart B, 0 (0, 4) stitches Chart A, 28 stitches Chart D, 26 stitches Chart E, 28 stitches Chart D, 0 (0, 4) stitches Chart C, 18 stitches Chart B, 2 (8, 10) stitches Chart A. Continue in patterns as established until 8 rows of Chart D have been worked 13 (14, 15) times. Piece measures approximately 13 (14, 15)" from beginning.

*Shape armholes*

Bind off 4 (4, 6) stitches at beginning of next 2 rows, 3 stitches at beginning of next 4 (6, 4) rows, 2 stitches at beginning of next 6 (4, 8) rows, 1 stitch at beginning of next 2 (4, 2) rows, AT SAME TIME, after 8 rows of Chart D have been worked from beginning of armhole shaping, replace it with 12 rows of Chart F, then continue with Chart G to end. Work even on 86 (94, 102) stitches until armhole measures 7½ (8, 8½)", end with row 4 of Chart G.

*Shape shoulders*

Bind off 6 (7, 8) stitches at beginning of next 6 rows, 7 (8, 9) stitches at beginning of next 2 rows. Bind off remaining 36 stitches.

## Left Front

Cast on 66 (72, 78) stitches. *Begin chart patterns: Row 1* (RS) Work 2 (8, 10) stitches Chart A, 18 stitches Chart B, 0 (0, 4) stitches Chart C, 28 stitches Chart D, 18 stitches Chart B. *Row 2* Work 18 stitches Chart B, 28 stitches Chart D, 0 (0, 4) stitches Chart C, 18 stitches Chart B, 2 (8, 10) stitches Chart A. Continue in patterns as established until piece measures same length as back to underarm, end with row 8 of Chart D.

*Shape armhole*

Shape armhole at beginning of RS rows as for back, AT SAME TIME, when 8 rows of Chart D have been worked from beginning of armhole shaping, replace it with Chart F, then Chart G as for back, and after row 12 of Chart B has been worked above armhole, replace it with Chart H. Work even on 47 (51, 55) stitches until armhole measures approximately 6½ (7, 7½)", end with row 1 of Chart G.

*Shape neck*

*Next row* (WS) Bind off 15 stitches (neck edge), work to end. Continue to bind off at beginning of every WS row 4 stitches once, 2 stitches once, 1 stitch once, AT SAME TIME, when armhole measures same length as back to shoulder, shape shoulder by binding off at beginning of RS rows 6 (7, 8) stitches 3 times, 7 (8, 9) stitches once.

Place markers along center front edge for 6 buttons, with the first 1" from lower edge, the last 1" from neck edge, and 4 others spaced evenly between.

## Right Front

**Note**: Work buttonholes opposite markers on right front as follows: On a RS row, work 4 stitches, yo, p2tog, work to end.

Cast on 66 (72, 78) stitches. *Begin chart patterns: Row 1* (RS) Work 18 stitches Chart B, 28 stitches Chart D, 0 (0, 4) stitches Chart C, 18 stitches Chart B, 2 (8, 10) stitches Chart C. *Row 2* Work 2 (8, 10) stitches Chart C, 18 stitches Chart B, 0 (0, 4) stitches Chart C, 28 stitches Chart D, 18 stitches Chart B. Continue in patterns as established until piece measures same length as back to underarm, end with row 1 of Chart D.

*Shape armhole*

Shape armhole at beginning of WS rows as for back, AT SAME TIME, when 8 rows of Chart D have been worked above armhole shaping, replace it with Chart F, then Chart G as for back, and after row 12 of Chart B has been worked above armhole, replace it with Chart I. Work even on 47 (51, 55) stitches until armhole measures approximately 6½ (7, 7½)", end with row 4 of Chart G. Shape neck at beginning of RS rows as for left front. When armhole measures same length as back to shoulder, shape shoulder at beginning of WS rows as for back.

## Sleeves

Cast on 58 (60, 64) stitches. *Begin chart patterns: Row 1* (RS) K2, then beginning Chart B as indicated, work to end of chart, work 28 stitches Chart D, work first 13 (14, 16) stitches of Chart B, ending as indicated, k2. Work patterns and increases simultaneously as follows: Work 2 repeats of Chart D, then replace it with 12 rows Chart F, then work Chart G to end, AT SAME TIME, when piece measures 3" from beginning, increase 1 stitch each side on next RS row, then every 8th row 11 (12, 13) times more—81 (85, 91) stitches. Work even until piece measures 15½ (16½, 17½)" from beginning, end with a WS row.

*Shape cap*

Bind off 3 stitches at beginning of next 2 rows, 2 stitches at beginning of next 2 rows. Decrease 1 stitch each side every RS row 15 (16, 17) times. Work 1 row even. Bind off 2 stitches at beginning of next 2 rows, 3 stitches at beginning of next 4 rows. Bind off remaining 25 (27, 31) stitches.

## Finishing

*Collar*

Cast on 76 stitches. Work Chart A for 2", end with a WS row. Bind off 3 stitches at beginning of next 10 rows. Bind off remaining 46 stitches.

Block pieces. Sew shoulders. Set in sleeves. Sew side and sleeve seams. Pin bound-off edge of collar around neck edge, beginning and ending 1" in from each edge. On each front, sew collar with WS of front facing so that seam is on underside of lapel when folded back. On back, sew collar with RS of back facing so seam is on inside of neck. Sew on buttons.

**Chart H**

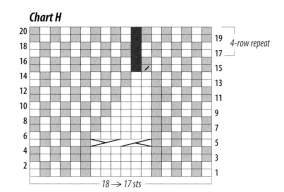

18 → 17 sts

**Chart I**

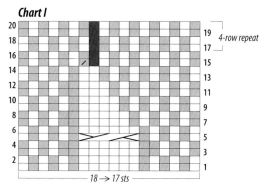

18 → 17 sts

**Chart A**

2-st repeat

**Chart B**

L M S    18 sts    S M L
end sleeve        beg sleeve

**Chart C**

2-st repeat

**Chart D**

28 sts

**Stitch key**

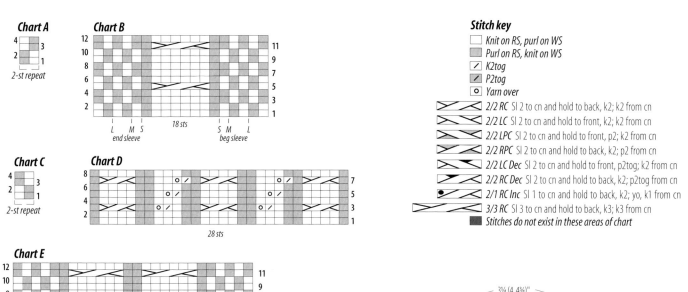

☐ Knit on RS, purl on WS
▨ Purl on RS, knit on WS
╱ K2tog
◪ P2tog
◉ Yarn over
2/2 RC Sl 2 to cn and hold to back, k2; k2 from cn
2/2 LC Sl 2 to cn and hold to front, k2; k2 from cn
2/2 LPC Sl 2 to cn and hold to front, p2; k2 from cn
2/2 RPC Sl 2 to cn and hold to back, k2; p2 from cn
2/2 LC Dec Sl 2 to cn and hold to front, p2tog; k2 from cn
2/2 RC Dec Sl 2 to cn and hold to back, k2; p2tog from cn
2/1 RC Inc Sl 1 to cn and hold to back, k2; yo, k1 from cn
3/3 RC Sl 3 to cn and hold to back, k3; k3 from cn
■ Stitches do not exist in these areas of chart

**Chart E**

26 sts

**Chart F**

28 → 30 → 27 sts

**Chart G**

27 sts

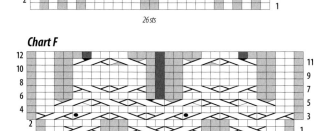

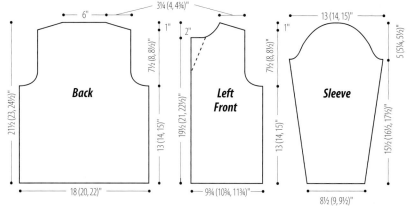

Back Pattern Arrangement

Back — 6"
3¼ (4, 4¾)"
1"
2"
7½ (8, 8½)"
19½ (21, 22½)"
13 (14, 15)"
21½ (23, 24½)"
18 (20, 22)"

Left Front
7½ (8, 8½)"
13 (14, 15)"
9¾ (10¾, 11¾)"

Sleeve
13 (14, 15)"
1"
5 (5¼, 5½)"
15½ (16½, 17½)"
8½ (9, 9½)"

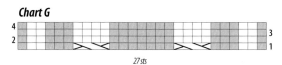

| 18 sts Chart B | 28 sts Chart D | 0(0,4) sts Chart C | 18 sts Chart B | 2(8,10) sts Chart A | 2(8,10) sts Chart C | 18 sts Chart B | 0(0,4) sts Chart A | 28 sts Chart D | 26 sts Chart E | 28 sts Chart D | 0(0,4) sts Chart C | 18 sts Chart B | 2(8,10) sts Chart A | 2(8,10) sts Chart C | 18 sts Chart B | 0(0,4) sts Chart C | 28 sts Chart D | 18 sts Chart B |
|---|---|---|---|---|---|---|---|---|---|---|---|---|---|---|---|---|---|---|

**Left Front Pattern Arrangement**

**Right Front Pattern Arrangement**

*If you're looking for a jacket that is a "suit-able" alternative for the office, you'll find a sophisticated one here. Simple lines and no frills make this easy-knitting project a wardrobe staple. The solid ecru yarn is linen and the variegated ribbon is rayon. What a great combination!*

Jean Frost

# on the neutral track

**INTERMEDIATE**

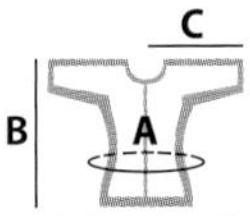

**STANDARD FIT**

**Sizes XS (S, M, L, 1X, 2X)**
**Shown in Small**
*A* 37 (40, 43, 45½, 48½, 51½)"
*B* 20¾ (20¾, 21¼, 22½, 23¾, 25)"
*C* 27½ (28, 29, 29½, 31½, 32)"

**10cm/4"**

38
22
• *over Chart Pattern*

1 2 3 **4** 5 6

• *Medium weight*
*A* • 685 (750, 800, 875, 1020, 1110) yds
*B* • 475 (520, 550, 610, 710, 770) yds

4mm/US 6, *or size to obtain gauge,*
74cm/29" long

• stitch holders
• stitch markers

*original yarn*

BERROCO Glace Colors (rayon; 50g; 75 yds) variegated (A)
Flax (linen; 50g; 65 yds) ecru (B)

## Notes

**1** See *School*, page 94, for 3-needle bind-off and long-tail cast-on. **2** Use long-tail cast-on throughout. **3** Work jacket in one piece to underarm, then divide for fronts and back. **4** Keep 1 stitch each side in garter stitch (knit every row) for selvage.

## Body

With A, cast on 201 (217, 233, 249, 265, 281) stitches. Knit 3 rows. Work 6 rows of Chart Pattern 19 (19, 20, 22, 23, 25) times. Piece measures approximately 12½ (12½, 13, 14¼, 15, 16¼)" from beginning.

*Divide for fronts and back*

**Next row** (RS) Work 44 (48, 52, 56, 60, 64) stitches (right front), bind off 13 stitches (underarm), work until there are 87 (95, 103, 111, 119, 127) stitches for back, bind off 13 stitches (underarm), work to end (left front). **Next row** (WS) Work 44 (48, 52, 56, 60, 64) stitches of left front and place remaining stitches on hold.

## Left Front

*Shape armhole*

Decrease 1 stitch at armhole edge every RS row 6 times—38 (42, 46, 50, 54, 58) stitches. Work even until 6 rows of chart have been worked 8 (8, 8, 8, 9, 9) times above underarm, then work Row 1 once more. Armhole measures approximately 5¼ (5¼, 5¼, 5¼, 5¾, 5¾)".

*Shape neck*

**Next row** (WS) Bind off 6 (6, 6, 6, 7, 7) stitches (neck edge), work to end. Continue to bind off at neck edge 3 (3, 3, 3, 4, 4) stitches once, 1 stitch 5 (5, 5, 5, 7, 7) times—24 (28, 32, 36, 36, 40) stitches. Work 16 (16, 16, 16, 12, 12) rows even, ending with chart row 6. Armhole measures approximately 8¼ (8¼, 8¼, 8¼, 8¾, 8¾)". Place stitches on hold.

## Right Front

With WS facing, join yarn at underarm and work as for left front, reversing shaping. Work armhole decreases at end of RS rows—38 (42, 46, 50, 54, 58) stitches. Work even

until 6 rows of chart have been worked 8 (8, 8, 8, 9, 9) times above underarm. Work neck bind-offs at beginning of RS rows. Work even until armhole measures same length as right front to shoulder. Place stitches on hold.

## Back

With WS facing, join yarn at underarm edge and shape armhole each side as for fronts—75 (83, 91, 99, 107, 115) stitches. Work even until armhole measures same length as fronts to shoulder. Place stitches on hold.

## Sleeves

With A, cast on 45 (53, 53, 53, 61, 61) stitches. Knit 3 rows. Work in Chart Pattern, AT SAME TIME, increase 1 stitch each side (working increases into pattern) on 7th row, then every 8th (8th, 8th, 6th, 6th, 6th) row 11 (11, 11, 4, 8, 8) times, every 10th (10th, 10th, 8th, 8th, 8th) row 4 (4, 4, 13, 10, 10) times—77 (85, 85, 89, 99, 99) stitches. Work 9 rows even, ending with chart row 6. Piece measures approximately 15½" from beginning.

*Shape cap*

Bind off 7 stitches at beginning of next 2 rows. Decrease 1 stitch each side on next row, then every other row 22 (18, 18, 16, 23, 23) times more. Work 1 row even. Bind off 2 stitches at beginning of next 0 (8, 8, 12, 10, 10) rows. Bind off remaining 17 stitches.

## Finishing

Block pieces. Join shoulders, using 3-needle bind-off, as follows: Join 24 (28, 32, 36, 36, 40) stitches of first shoulder, bind off back neck stitches until 24 (28, 32, 36, 36, 40) stitches remain, then join 2nd shoulder.

*Neck edging*

With RS facing and A, pick up and knit 71 (71, 71, 71, 83, 83) stitches evenly around neck edge. Knit 3 rows. Bind off.

*Front edgings*

With RS facing and A, pick up and knit 78 (78, 82, 92, 102, 112) stitches along each front edge. Knit 3 rows. Bind off. Set in sleeves. Sew sleeve seams.

**Chart Pattern**

4-st repeat

**Color key**
■ A
□ B

**Stitch key**
□ Knit on RS, purl on WS
– Knit on WS
Ⅴ Sl 1 purlwise with yarn at WS of work

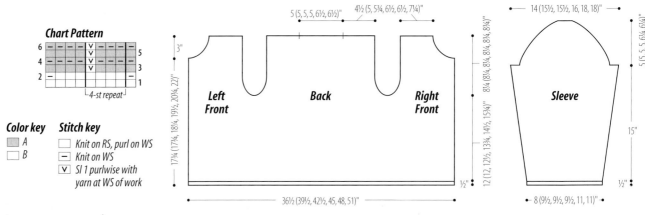

Left Front    Back    Right Front    Sleeve

5 (5, 5, 5, 6½, 6½)"    4½ (5, 5¾, 6½, 6½, 7¼)"    14 (15½, 15½, 16, 18, 18)"

3"

17¾ (17¾, 18¼, 19½, 20¾, 22)"

8¼ (8¼, 8¼, 8¼, 8¾, 8¾)"

12 (12, 12½, 13¾, 14½, 15¾)"

½"

15"

5 (5, 5, 5, 6¼, 6¼)"

½"

36½ (39½, 42½, 45, 48, 51)"    8 (9½, 9½, 9½, 11, 11)"

*With this jacket, you'll get both pleasurable knitting and a wearable finished product in the process. Twisted-stitch patterns and an easy shape go hand in hand to make this piece a classic.*

Norah Gaughan

# breaktime beauty

**INTERMEDIATE**

**STANDARD FIT**

**Sizes S (M, L/1X, 2X/3X)**
**Shown in Medium**
A 38¼ (43¾, 49¾, 55½)"
B 20¾ (20¾, 22, 23)"
C 27½ (29, 30½, 32)"

**10cm/4"**
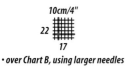
22
17
• over Chart B, using larger needles

1 2 3 **4** 5 6

• *Medium weight*
1175 (1310, 1535, 1770) yds

5mm/US 8 and 6mm/US 10,
*or size to obtain gauge*

• 5 (5, 5, 6) 22mm/⅞"

• stitch holders
• stitch markers

*original yarn*
JCA/REYNOLDS Dover
(wool; 50g; 82 yds)
Claret

## Back

With smaller needles, cast on 80 (92, 104, 116) stitches. Purl 2 rows. Change to larger needles. Work Chart A for 16 rows. *Begin Chart B: Row 1* (RS) K6 (1, 2, 8), then beginning as indicated for back, work chart pattern to last 6 (1, 2, 8) stitches, ending as indicated for back, k6 (1, 2, 8). Continue in pattern as established, keeping first and last 6 (1, 2, 8) stitches in stockinette stitch (St st), until 36 rows of chart have been worked twice, then work first 14 (14, 20, 20) rows once more. Work in St st over all stitches until piece measures 19¾ (19¾, 21, 22)" from beginning, end with a WS row. *Begin Chart C: Row 1* (RS) K2, work 4-stitch repeat to last 2 stitches, k2. Work through chart row 6, keeping first and last 2 stitches in St st. Bind off.

## Left Front

With smaller needles, cast on 46 (54, 60, 66) stitches. Purl 2 rows. Change to larger needles. Work Chart A for 16 rows. *Begin Chart B: Row 1* (RS) K6 (1, 2, 8), then beginning as indicated for left front, work chart pattern to last 9 (11, 11, 11) stitches, then work Chart A to end, beginning with 2nd stitch of chart. Continue in pattern as established until piece measures 17¾ (17¾, 18½, 19½)" from beginning, end with a RS row.

*Shape neck*

*Next row* *(WS)* Work 9 (11, 11, 11) stitches and place them on hold (neck edge), work to end. Continue in pattern, AT SAME TIME, bind off at neck edge (beginning of WS rows) 4 stitches 0 (1, 1, 1) time, 3 stitches 2 (2, 1, 3) times, 2 stitches 2 (1, 3, 1) times—27 (31, 36, 40) stitches. Work even until piece measures same length as back to Chart C, end with a WS row. *Begin Chart C: Row 1* (RS) K2, work 4-stitch repeat 6 (7, 8, 9) times, k1 (1, 2, 2). Work through chart row 6, keeping stitches each side in St st. Bind off. Place markers for 5 (5, 5, 6) buttons along left front edge, with the first ½" from neck edge, the last 1" from lower edge and 3 (3, 3, 4) others spaced evenly between.

## Right Front

(**Note** Work buttonholes on WS rows opposite markers as follows: Purl to last 5 (7, 7, 7) stitches, yo, p2tog, purl to end.)

Work as for left front through 16 rows of Chart A, working 1 buttonhole opposite left front marker. *Begin Chart B: Row 1* (RS) Work Chart A as established over 9 (11, 11, 11) stitches, then beginning as indicated for right front, work chart pattern to last 6 (1, 2, 8) stitches, ending as indicated, k6 (1, 2, 8). Complete to correspond to left front, reversing neck shaping, and working buttonholes. Work Chart C as follows: *Row 1* (RS) K1 (1, 2, 2), work 4-stitch repeat 6 (7, 8, 9) times, k2.

## Sleeves

With smaller needles, cast on 44 (48, 52, 56) stitches. Purl 2 rows. Change to larger needles. Work Chart A for 12 rows. Beginning and ending as indicated for sleeve, work Chart B through row 20, then work in St st, AT SAME TIME, increase 1 stitch each side (working increases into pattern), on 5th (5th, 3rd, 3rd) chart row, then every 6th (6th, 4th, 4th) row 9 (9, 3, 18) times, every 8th (8th, 6th, 0) row 2 (2, 10, 0) times—68 (72, 80, 94) stitches. Work even until piece measures 17¼" from beginning, end with a WS row. *Begin Chart C: Row 1* (RS) K2 (2, 2, 1), work 4-stitch repeat 16 (17, 19, 23) times, k2 (2, 2, 1). Work through row 6, keeping 2 (2, 2, 1) stitches each side in St st. Bind off.

## Finishing

Block pieces. Sew shoulders. Place markers 8 (8½, 9½, 11)" down from shoulders on front and back for armholes. Sew sleeves between markers. Sew side and sleeve seams.

*Neckband*

With RS facing and smaller needles, k9 (11, 11, 11) stitches from right front holder, pick up and knit 70 (74, 80, 84) stitches evenly around neck edge to left front holder, k9 (11, 11, 11) stitches from holder—88 (96, 102, 106) stitches. Knit 1 row. Purl 1 row. Bind off knitwise.

*Front edgings*

With RS facing and smaller needles, pick up and knit 80 (80, 84, 88) stitches evenly along each front edge. Bind off knitwise. Sew on buttons.

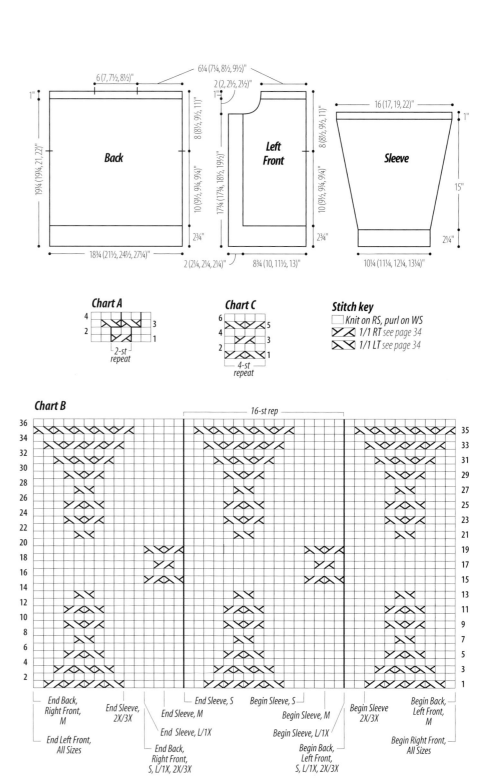

## Back
1"
19¾ (19¾, 21, 22)"
6 (7, 7½, 8½)"
6¼ (7¼, 8½, 9½)"
8 (8½, 9½, 11)"
10 (9½, 9¾, 9¼)"
2¾"
18¾ (21½, 24½, 27¼)"

## Left Front
2 (2, 2½, 2½)"
1"
8 (8½, 9½, 11)"
17¾ (17¾, 18½, 19½)"
10 (9½, 9¾, 9¼)"
2¾"
2 (2¼, 2¼, 2¼)"
8¾ (10, 11½, 13)"

## Sleeve
16 (17, 19, 22)"
1"
15"
2¼"
10¼ (11¼, 12¼, 13¼)"

### Chart A
4
2
3
1
2-st repeat

### Chart C
6
4
2
5
3
1
4-st repeat

### Stitch key
☐ Knit on RS, purl on WS
◤◥ 1/1 RT see page 34
◤◥ 1/1 LT see page 34

### Chart B
16-st rep

36 34 32 30 28 26 24 22 20 18 16 14 12 10 8 6 4 2
35 33 31 29 27 25 23 21 19 17 15 13 11 9 7 5 3 1

End Back, Right Front, M
End Sleeve, 2X/3X
End Left Front, All Sizes
End Sleeve, M
End Sleeve, L/1X
End Back, Right Front, S, L/1X, 2X/3X
End Sleeve, S
Begin Sleeve, S
Begin Sleeve, M
Begin Sleeve, L/1X
Begin Back, Left Front, S, L/1X, 2X/3X
Begin Sleeve 2X/3X
Begin Back, Left Front, M
Begin Right Front, All Sizes

# HOW TO:

### 1/1 RIGHT TWIST (1/1 RT)

 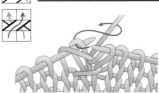 

*1* Bring right needle *in front of* first stitch on left needle. Knit second stitch but *do not remove* it from left needle.

*2* Knit first stitch.

*3* Pull both stitches off left needle. Completed 1/1 RT: 1 stitch crosses over 1 stitch and to the right.

### 1/1 LEFT TWIST (1/1 LT)

*1* Bring right needle *behind* first stitch on left needle, and *to front between* first and second stitches. Knit second stitch, but *do not remove* it from left needle.

*2* Bring right needle to right and in front of first stitch and knit first stitch.

*3* Pull both stitches off left needle. Completed 1/1 LT: 1 stitch crosses over 1 stitch and to the left.

Jean Frost

# brocade in charcoal

**INTERMEDIATE**

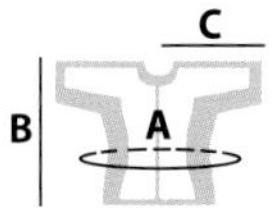

**LOOSE FIT**

**Sizes S (M, L, 1X, 2X)**
**Shown in Medium**
A 40¼ (43¾, 46, 50¾, 53)"
B 21¼ (21¾, 22¾, 24¾, 25¾)"
C 27½ (29, 30, 31, 32)"

**10cm/4"**

31

20
• over chart pattern

1 2 3 **4** 5 6

• Medium weight
1305 (1425, 1580, 1810, 1910) yds

• 4mm/US 6,
or size to obtain gauge

• five 16mm/⅝"

**&**

• stitch holders
• stitch markers

**original yarn**
CASCADE Lana de Oro (alpaca
blend; 50g; 110 yds) gray
Reknit: CASCADE 220 (wool;
100g; 220 yds) gray

## Notes

**1** See *School*, page 94 for SSK, S2KP2 and 3-needle bind-off. **2** Knit first and last stitch of every row for selvage.

## Back

Cast on 93 (105, 111, 123, 129) stitches. **Work reverse stockinette stitch (rev St st) band: Rows 1 and 3** (WS) Knit. *Row 2* K1, purl to last stitch, k1. **Begin Chart Pattern: Row 1** (RS) K1 (selvage), then beginning as indicated for back, work chart pattern to last stitch, ending as indicated, k1 (selvage). Continue in chart pattern as established until piece measures 14 (14, 14½, 15½, 16)" from beginning, end with a WS row.
*Shape armholes*
Bind off 6 (7, 7, 9, 9) stitches at beginning of next 2 rows. **Decrease row** (RS) K1, k2tog, work to last 3 stitches, SSK, k1. Repeat decrease row every RS row 4 (5, 5, 6, 7) times more—71 (79, 85, 91, 95) stitches. Work even until armhole measures 6½ (7, 7½, 8½, 9)". Place stitches on hold.

## Right Front

Cast on 54 (56, 59, 65, 68) stitches. Work 3-row rev St st band as for back. **Begin Chart Pattern: Row 1** (RS) K1, then beginning as indicated for right front, work chart pattern to last stitch, ending as indicated, k1. Continue in pattern as established until piece measures 12½ (12½, 13, 14, 14½)" from beginning, end with a WS row.
*Shape V-neck and armhole*
**Decrease row** (RS) K1, k2tog (neck edge), work to end. Continue to decrease 1 stitch at neck edge every other row 4 (0, 0, 0, 0) times, every 4th row 15 (14, 12, 11, 13) times, every 6th row 0 (3, 5, 7, 6) times, AT SAME TIME, when piece measures same length as back to underarm, shape armhole at beginning of a WS row and at end of RS rows as for back—23 (25, 28, 30, 31) stitches. Work even until armhole measures 8¼ (8¾, 9¼, 10¼, 10¾)". Place stitches on hold.

## Left Front

Work as for right front, reversing shaping, and beginning and ending chart as indicated for left front. Work neck decreases by working SSK, k1 at end of RS rows. Shape armhole at beginning of RS rows.

## Sleeves

Cast on 51 (51, 57, 57, 57) stitches. Work 3-row rev St st band as for back. **Begin Chart Pattern: Row 1** (RS) K1, then beginning and ending as indicated for sleeve, work chart pattern to last stitch, ending as indicated, k1. Continue in pattern as established, AT SAME TIME, increase 1 stitch each side (working increases into pat-

tern) on 7th row, then every 8th (8th, 8th, 6th, 6th) row 5 (10, 10, 6, 10) times, then every 10th (10th, 10th, 8th, 8th) row 6 (2, 2, 8, 5) times—75 (77, 83, 87, 89) stitches. Work even until piece measures 15½" from beginning, end with a WS row.
*Shape cap*
Bind off 6 (7, 7, 9, 9) stitches at beginning of next 2 rows. Decrease 1 stitch each side of every RS row 18 (19, 21, 24, 25) times. Work 1 row even. Bind off 3 (2, 3, 0, 0) stitches at beg of next 2 (2, 2, 0, 0) rows. Bind off remaining 21 stitches.

## Collar

**Collar pattern** *OVER 16 STITCHES*
*Row 1* (RS) [Yo, k1] twice, yo, [SSK] twice, S2KP2, [k2tog] twice, [yo, k1] 3 times.
*Row 2* Purl. *Row 3* Knit. *Row 4* Purl. Repeat rows 1–4 for collar pattern.
Cast on 163 (177, 185, 201, 205) stitches. Work 3-row rev St st band as for back. **Next row** (RS) Bind off 1 stitch, knit until there are 17 (16, 20, 20, 22) stitches on right needle, place marker (pm), work row 1 of collar pattern 8 (9, 9, 10, 10) times, pm, knit to end. Continue working St st (knit on RS, purl on WS) at each side, and collar pattern between markers, for 15 rows more, then continue in St st over all stitches, AT SAME TIME, bind off 1 stitch at beginning of next 9 rows, 3 (4, 5, 6, 6) stitches at beginning of next 8 (8, 10, 8, 4) rows, 4 (5, 0, 8, 7) stitches at beginning of next 2 (2, 0, 2, 6) rows, 16 stitches at beginning of next 6 rows. Bind off remaining 25 (29, 29, 31, 33) stitches.

## Finishing

Block pieces. Join shoulders, using 3-needle bind-off as follows: join 23 (25, 28, 30, 31) stitches of first shoulder, bind off back neck stitches until 23 (25, 28, 30, 31) stitches remain, join 2nd shoulder.
*Left front band*
With RS facing, begin at first V-neck decrease and pick up and knit 66 (66, 68, 72, 74) stitches evenly to lower edge. *Rows 1 and 3* (WS) Knit. *Row 2* Purl. Bind off purlwise.
*Right front band*
Place markers for 5 buttonholes along right front edge as follows: The first 2½" below first V-neck decrease, the last 3 (3, 3½, 3½, 4)" from lower edge, and 3 others evenly spaced between. With RS facing, begin at lower edge and pick up and knit 66 (66, 68, 72) stitches along right front edge to first V-neck decrease, working buttonholes at each marker as follows: pick up and knit 1 stitch [pass 2nd stitch on right needle over first, pick up and knit 1 stitch] 3 times. On next row, cast on 3 stitches over the bound off ones.
With WS of collar facing RS of jacket, pin collar around neck edge. Sew in place. Sew edges of collar band to front bands. Set in sleeves. Sew side and sleeve seams. Sew on buttons.

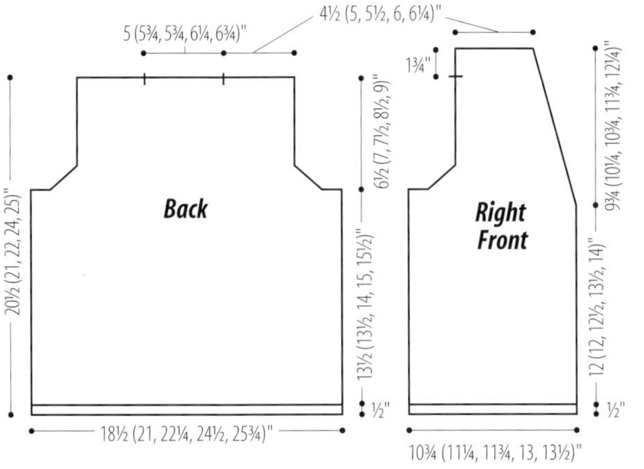
Back
Right Front
5 (5¾, 5¾, 6¼, 6¾)"
4½ (5, 5½, 6, 6¼)"
1¾"
20½ (21, 22, 24, 25)"
6½ (7, 7½, 8½, 9)"
13½ (13½, 14, 15, 15½)"
½"
9¾ (10¼, 10¾, 11¾, 12¼)"
12 (12, 12½, 13½, 14)"
½"
18½ (21, 22¼, 24½, 25¾)"
10¾ (11¼, 11¾, 13, 13½)"

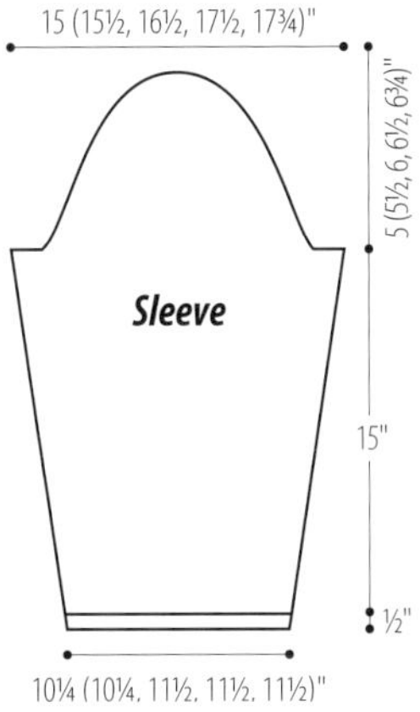
Sleeve
15 (15½, 16½, 17½, 17¾)"
5 (5½, 6, 6½, 6¾)"
15"
½"
10¼ (10¼, 11½, 11½, 11½)"

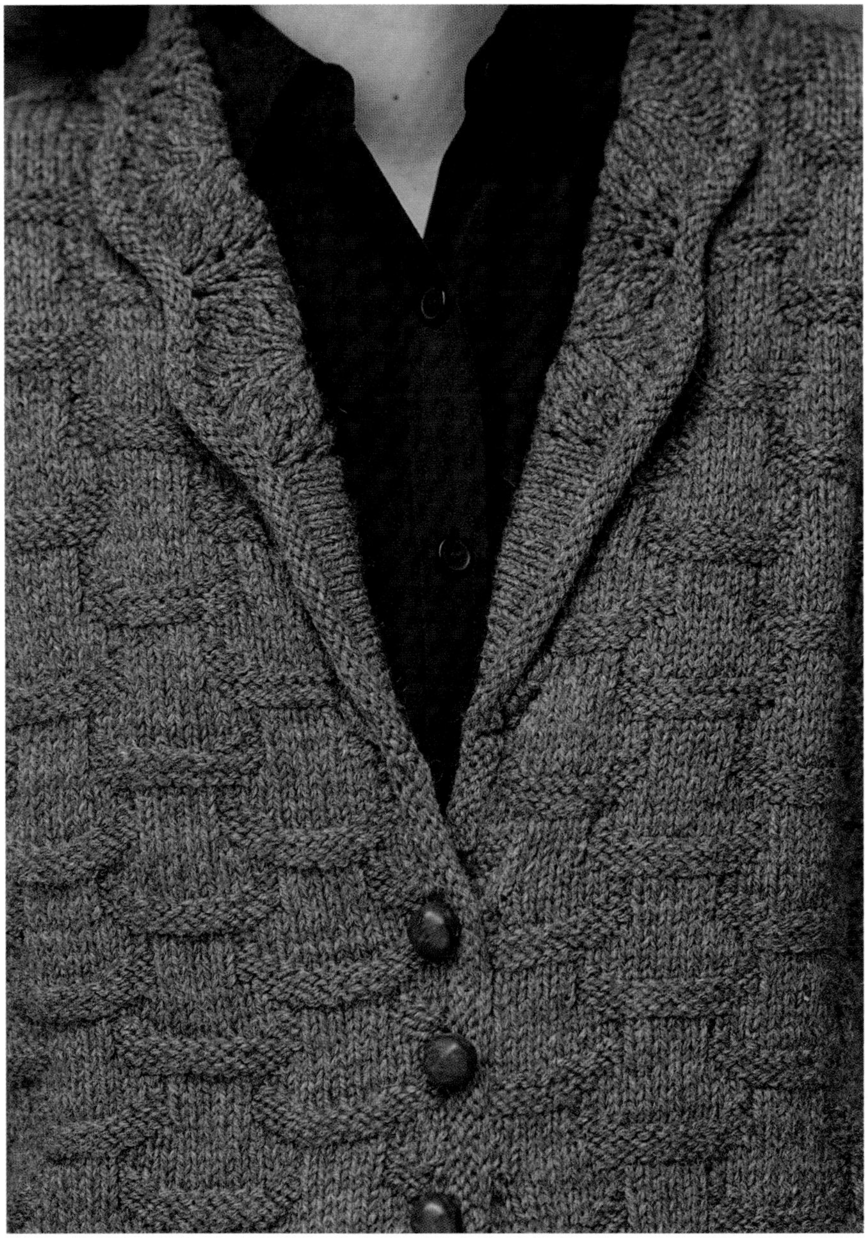

**Chart Pattern**

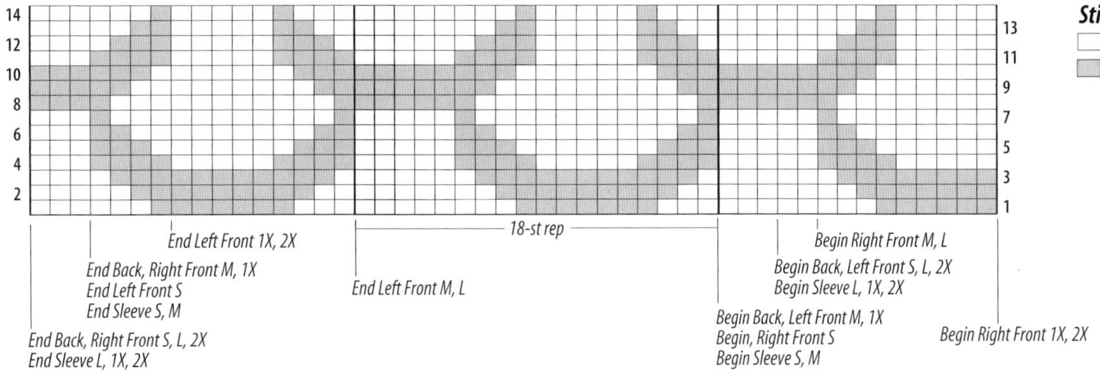
14
12
10
8
6
4
2
13
11
9
7
5
3
1
18-st rep
End Left Front 1X, 2X
End Back, Right Front M, 1X
End Left Front S
End Sleeve S, M
End Back, Right Front S, L, 2X
End Sleeve L, 1X, 2X
End Left Front M, L
Begin Right Front M, L
Begin Back, Left Front S, L, 2X
Begin Sleeve L, 1X, 2X
Begin Back, Left Front M, 1X
Begin, Right Front S
Begin Sleeve S, M
Begin Right Front 1X, 2X

**Stitch key**

- *Knit on RS, purl on WS*
- *Purl on RS, knit on WS*

This tailored suit has many knitted details that are quick to master and really show off a knitter's skill. The traveling cables form flattering mock princess lines, the front edges have a modified I-cord knit-on trim that finishes the edge cleanly and unobtrusively.

*Linda Cyr*

# mauve power suit

**ADVANCED**

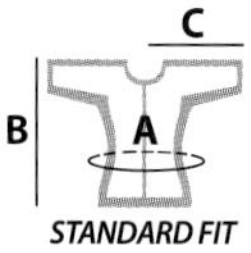

**STANDARD FIT**
**Sizes XS (S, M, L)**
**Shown in Small**
A 33½ (36, 40, 42½)"
B 21 (22, 23, 24)"
C 28 (29, 30, 31)"

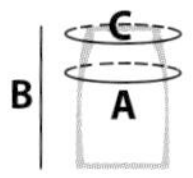

**LOOSE FIT**
A 34½ (36½, 40½, 42½)"
B 21 (21, 21, 21)"
C 24¼ (25¼, 27¼, 29¼)"

10cm/4"
32
24
• over moss stitch, using smaller
needles and MC

1 2 3 **4** 5 6
• Medium weight
MC • 1925 (2110, 2430, 2670) yds

1 2 3 4 **5** 6
• Bulky weight
CC • 90 (99, 115, 125) yds

• 3.5mm/US 4 and 6mm/US 10,
or size to obtain gauge

• seven 23mm/⅞"

• 7" zipper
• 1 yd ¾" elastic
• stitch markers

**Notes 1** See School, page 94, for 1-row buttonhole. **2** Slip stitches purlwise with yarn at WS of work.

**Moss stitch** (over an even number of stitches)
**Row 1** (RS) * K1, p1; repeat from *. **Rows 2 and 4** Knit the knit stitches and purl the purl stitches. **Row 3** * P1, k1; repeat from *. Repeat rows 1–4 for moss stitch.

**Right Cable (RC) pattern** (over 8 stitches)
**Rows 1, 3 and 7** (RS) P1, k6, p1. **Rows 2, 4, 6 and 8** K1, p6, k1. **Row 5** P1, slip (sl) 3 to cn, hold to back, k3; k3 from cn, p1. Repeat rows 1–8 for RC pattern.

**Left Cable (LC) pattern** (over 8 stitches)
**Rows 1, 3 and 7** (RS) P1, k6, p1. **Rows 2, 4, 6 and 8** K1, p6, k1. **Row 5** P1, sl 3 to cn, hold to front, k3; k3 from cn, p1. Repeat rows 1–8 for LC pattern.

**Right Traveling Cable over 1 (RTC1) pattern**
Work as for RC pattern, except work **Row 5** as follows (pattern shifts 1 stitch to right on this row): P1, sl 4 to cn, hold to back, k3; [k3, p1] from cn.

**Left Traveling Cable over 1 (LTC1) pattern**
Work as for LC pattern, except work **Row 5** as follows (pattern shifts 1 stitch to left on this row): Sl 3 to cn, hold to front, p1, k3; k3 from cn, p1.

**Right Traveling Cable over 2 (RTC2) pattern**
Work as for RC pattern, except work **Row 5** as follows (pattern shifts 2 stitches to right on this row): P1, sl 5 to cn, hold to back, k3; sl 5 stitches from cn to left needle and k3, p1 (last stitch slipped from cn will be worked into center moss stitch pattern).

**Left Traveling Cable over 2 (LTC2) pattern**
Work as for LC pattern, except work **Row 5** as follows (pattern shifts 2 stitches to left on this row): Sl 3 to cn, hold to front, work next stitch into moss stitch (1 more stitch added to center panel), p1, k3; k3 from cn, p1.

## JACKET

### Back

With smaller needles and MC, cast on 104 (110, 122, 128) stitches. Work in k1, p1 rib for 4 rows. **Begin RC and LC patterns: Row 1** (RS) Work 28 (30, 34, 36) stitches in moss stitch, 8 stitches RC pattern, 32 (34, 38, 40) stitches in moss stitch, 8 stitches LC pattern, 28 (30, 34, 36) stitches in moss stitch. Continue in patterns as established until 8 rows of pattern have been worked 10 times. **Begin RTC1 and LTC1 patterns** Work patterns as established for 4 rows, then work as follows: **Row 5** (RS) Work 27 (29, 33, 35) stitches in moss stitch (ending 1 stitch before cable pattern), work row 5 of RTC1 pattern, work 34 (36, 40, 42) stitches in moss stitch (ending 1 stitch into cable pattern),

work row 5 of LTC1 pattern, work 27 (29, 33, 35) stitches in moss stitch. Continue in patterns as established, shifting cable patterns 1 stitch to right and left on every pattern row 5 (working 1 stitch less in moss stitch on side panels and 2 stitches more in center panel), AT SAME TIME, after 92 (96, 104, 108) rows have been worked from beginning and piece measures approximately 12 (12½, 13½, 14)", shape armholes.

*Shape armholes*
Bind off 5 stitches at beginning of next 2 rows. Decrease 1 stitch each side every RS row 3 (4, 5, 5) times—88 (92, 102, 108) stitches. Work 21 (15, 5, 1) rows even, ending with row 8 of cable pattern. There are 15 (16, 19, 21) moss stitches at sides and 42 (44, 48, 50) stitches in center. **Begin RTC2 and LTC2 patterns** Work patterns as established for 4 rows, then work as follows: **Row 5** (RS) Work 13 (14, 17, 19) stitches in moss stitch (ending 2 stitches before cable pattern), work row 5 of RTC2 pattern, work 45 (47, 51, 53) stitches in moss stitch (ending 1 stitch into cable pattern), work row 5 of LTC2 pattern, work 13 (14, 17, 19) stitches in moss stitch. There are 13 (14, 17, 19) moss stitches at sides and 46 (48, 52, 54) stitches in center. Continue in patterns as established for 7 rows more, ending with pattern row 4. **Row 5** (RS) Work 11 (12, 15, 17) stitches in moss stitch (ending 2 stitches before cable pattern), work row 5 of RTC2 pattern, work 49 (51, 55, 57) stitches in moss stitch (ending 1 stitch into cable pattern), work row 5 of LTC2 pattern, work 11 (12, 15, 17) stitches in moss stitch. There are 11 (12, 15, 17) moss stitches at sides and 50 (52, 56, 58) stitches in center. Continue in patterns as established, shifting cables 2 stitches every pattern row 5 (working 2 fewer stitches in moss stitch on side panels and 4 more stitches in center panel) until a total of 156 (164, 172, 180) rows have been worked from beginning. Armhole measures approximately 8 (8½, 8½, 9)". There are 7 (6, 7, 7) moss stitches at sides and 58 (64, 72, 78) stitches in center.
*Shape shoulders*
Bind off 5 (5, 6, 6) stitches at beginning of next 8 rows. Bind off remaining 48 (52, 54, 60) stitches.

### Left Front

With smaller needles and MC, cast on 57 (61, 67, 71) stitches. **Begin edging and k1, p1 rib pattern: Row 1** (RS) Work in k1, p1 rib to last 3 stitches, sl 3. **Rows 2 and 4** [P1, yo] twice, p1, work in rib pattern to end. **Row 3** Work in rib pattern to last 5 stitches, [sl 1, drop yo] twice, sl 1. **Begin RC pattern: Row 1** (RS) Work 28 (30, 34, 36) stitches in moss stitch, 8 stitches RC pattern, 18 (20, 22, 24) stitches in moss stitch, [sl 1, drop yo] twice, sl 1. **Row 2** [P1, yo] twice, p1, work 18 (20, 22, 24) stitches in moss stitch, 8 stitches RC pattern, 28 (30, 34, 36) stitches in moss stitch. Continue in patterns as established until 80 rows have been worked above ribbing. Work RTC1 pattern in place of RC pattern for 40 rows, then work RTC2 pattern, AT

*original yarn*

PAUA FIBERS/SILKWOOD DESIGNER YARNS Sensations (kid mohair; alpaca; wool; 50g; 111 yds) mulberry (MC)
SILKWOOD Legends (kid mohair; wool; silk; 50g; 99 yds) wine (CC)

SAME TIME, shape armhole at beginning of RS rows as for back—49 (52, 57, 61) stitches. Work 17 (15, 11, 11) rows even. Armhole measures approximately 3 (3, 2¾, 2¾ )".

*Shape neck*

**Note:** Work decreases before edging on RS rows and after edging on WS rows.

* Decrease 1 stitch at neck edge every row twice, work 1 row even; repeat from * 6 (8, 8, 12) times more, then decrease 1 stitch every other row 12 (11, 12, 8) times, AT SAME TIME, when armhole measures same length as back to shoulder, shape shoulder at beginning of RS rows as for back. Continue working edging on remaining 3 stitches until piece, slightly stretched, fits to center back neck. Bind off. Place 5 markers for buttons along center front edge, with the first at beginning of neck shaping, the last at top of ribbing and 3 others spaced evenly between.

### Right Front

With smaller needles and MC, cast on 57 (61, 67, 71) stitches. *Begin edging and k1, p1 rib pattern: Row 1* (RS) [K1, yo] twice, k1, work in k1, p1 rib to end. *Row 2* Work in rib pattern to last 5 stitches, [sl 1, drop yo] twice, sl 1, work in rib pattern to end. *Rows 3 and 4* Repeat rows 1 and 2. *Begin LC pattern: Row 1* (RS) Work edging, then work 18 (20, 22, 24) stitches in moss stitch, 8 stitches LC pattern, 28 (30, 34, 36) stitches in moss stitch. Work to correspond to left front, reversing shaping and working left cable patterns, AT SAME TIME, work buttonholes on RS rows to correspond to button markers as follows: Work 5 stitches, work 5-stitch 1-row buttonhole, work to end.

### Sleeves

With smaller needles and MC, cast on 48 (52, 54, 54) stitches. Work 4 rows in k1, p1 rib. Work in moss stitch, AT SAME TIME, increase 1 stitch each side (working increases into pattern) on 7th row, then every 6th (6th, 4th, 4th) row 13 (15, 1, 1) times, every 8th (8th, 6th, 6th) row 4 (3, 19, 19) times—84 (90, 96, 96) stitches. Work even until piece measures 16 (16½, 17, 17)" from beginning, end with a WS row.

*Shape cap*

Bind off 5 stitches at beginning of next 2 rows. Decrease 1 stitch each side every row 9 times, then every other row 13 (13, 10, 12) times, then every row 3 (3, 9, 7) times. Bind off remaining 24 (30, 30, 30) stitches.

### Collar

With larger needles and CC, cast on 78 (84, 86, 94) stitches. *Row 1* K27 (27, 28, 29), place marker (pm), [k8 (10, 10, 12), pm] 3 times, k27 (27, 28, 29). *Row 2* Knit. *Row 3* Knit, increasing 1 stitch before each of first 2 markers and after each of last 2 markers—82 (88, 90, 98) stitches. [Repeat rows 2 and 3] 9 times more—118 (124, 126, 134) stitches. Bind off.

### Cuffs (make 2)

With larger needles and CC, cast on 34 (36, 38, 38) stitches. *Rows 1 and 2* Knit. *Row 3* Increase 1, knit to end. *Row 4* Knit. [Repeat rows 2 and 3] 8 (8, 9, 9) times more—43 (45, 48, 48) stitches. Bind off.

### Finishing

Block pieces. Sew shoulders. Sew front edgings along back neck to center. Set in sleeves. Sew side and sleeve seams. Sew on buttons. With jacket buttoned, pin collar in place (begin and end approximately ½" from button) and block lightly. Sew collar to inside of neck edging, easing to fit. Sew cast-on edge of cuff along lower edge of sleeve, matching center point of cuff to sleeve seam. Fold cuff to RS of sleeve and tack straight edge along center of sleeve. Sew button on cuff's shaped edge, sewing through all 3 thicknesses.

### SKIRT

### Front

With smaller needles and MC, cast on 104 (110, 122, 128) stitches. Work 4 rows in k1, p1 rib. *Begin RC and LC patterns: Row 1* (RS) Work 28 (30, 34, 36) stitches in moss stitch, 8 stitches RC pattern, 32 (34, 38, 40) stitches in moss stitch, 8 stitches LC pattern, 28 (30, 34, 36) stitches in moss stitch. Work until piece measures 13" from beginning, end with a WS row.

*Shape hip*

Decrease 1 stitch each side on next row, then every 6th row 3 (2, 1, 1) times more, every 4th row 7 times, every other row 3 (5, 9, 9) times—76 (80, 86, 92) stitches. Work even until piece measures 21" from beginning, end with a WS row. Purl 2 rows for turning ridge. Work in stockinette stitch for 1" for casing. Bind off.

### Left Back

With smaller needles and MC, cast on 56 (58, 64, 68) stitches. Work in k1, p1 rib for 4 rows. *Begin LC pattern: Row 1* (RS) Work 20 (20, 22, 24) stitches in moss stitch, 8 stitches LC pattern, 28 (30, 34, 36) stitches in moss stitch. Continue in patterns as established until piece measures 6" from beginning, end with a WS row.

*Back vent*

*Next row* (RS) Bind off 2 stitches, work to end—54 (56, 62, 66) stitches. Work even until piece measures 13" from beginning, end with a WS row. Shape hip as for front, working decreases at end of RS rows—40 (41, 44, 48) stitches. Complete as for front.

### Right Back

With smaller needles and MC, cast on 56 (58, 64, 68) stitches. Work in k1, p1 rib for 4 rows. *Begin RC pattern: Row 1* (RS) Work 28 (30, 34, 36) stitches in moss stitch, 8 stitches RC pattern, 20 (20, 22, 24) stitches in moss stitch. Work as for left back, binding off for vent at beginning of a WS row and reversing hip shaping by decreasing at beginning of RS rows.

### Finishing

Block pieces. Sew left and right back along center seam from vent (overlapping vent) to approximately 7" from turning ridge. Sew in zipper. Sew side seams. Fold casing at turning ridge and sew to WS. Cut elastic to a comfortable waist measurement. Join safety pin to one end of elastic and slip through casing. Sew ends of elastic to zipper. Sew side edges of casing to zipper. *Optional:* Sew hook-and-eye to top of waistband at center back.

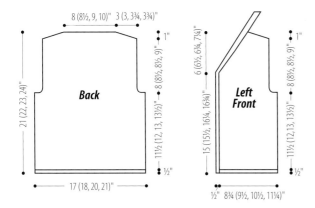

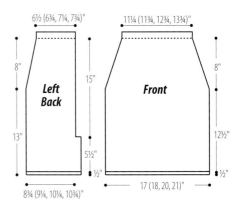

*We offer this jacket in yarns of very different weight—the body shape and the one-button detail remained the same. The split leaf pattern and fashionable colors were the ideal choices for this design.*

Stephanie Gildersleeve

## INTERMEDIATE

**VERSION 1**

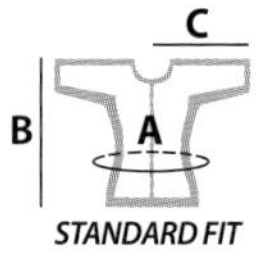

**STANDARD FIT**

**VERSION 2**

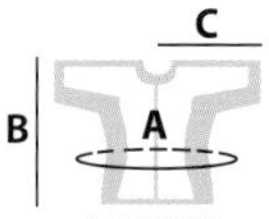

**LOOSE FIT**

**Sizes S (M, L)**
**Shown in Small**
**Version 1**
A 34¾ (39¼, 43¼)"
B 16½ (18½, 19½)"
C 24 (26, 28)"
**Version 2**
A 38¼ (44¼, 50¼)"
B 17 (18½, 19½)"
C 26 (27½, 30)"

**10cm/4"**
**40/25**
**23/16**
Version 1• over Split Leaf chart
Version 2• over Split Leaf chart

1 2 **3** 4 5 6

**Version 1 • Light weight**
1210 (1425, 1620) yds

1 2 3 **4** 5 6

**Version 2 • Medium weight**
Jacket • 800 (950, 1065) yds
Vest • 485 (620, 730) yds

**Version 1 • 3.5mm/US 4,**
**Version 2 • 5mm/US 8, or size to**
**obtain gauge**

**Version 1 • one 28mm/1⅛"**
**Version 2 • one 25mm/1"**

# two-way lace

## Notes

**1** See *School*, page 94, for SSK. **2** Instructions for Version 1 are given first; instructions for Version 2 follow in brackets. If there is only one figure or set of instructions, it applies to both versions. For ease in working, circle the numbers for your size. **3** Yarn overs (yo) in Split Leaf chart must be paired with decreases to maintain stitch count. If a decrease is omitted during shaping, omit the matching yo as well. **4** Work selvage stitches in stockinette stitch (knit on RS, purl on WS).

## Back

Cast on 99 (111, 123) [75, 87, 99] stitches. *Begin Chart Pattern: Row 1* (RS) K1 (selvage stitch), then beginning as indicated for back, work chart pattern to last stitch, ending chart as indicated, k1 (selvage stitch). Continue in pattern as established until piece measures 8½ (9½, 10) [8½, 9½, 10]" from beginning, end with a WS row.
*Shape armholes*
Bind off 5 [4] stitches at beginning of next 2 rows. Work 2 rows even. *Decrease row* (RS) K2, SSK, work in pattern to last 4 stitches, k2tog, k2. Repeat decrease row every 4th row 2 [0] times more, every other row 3 [2] times—77 (89, 101) [61, 73, 85] stitches. Work even until armhole measures 8 (9, 9½) [8½, 9, 9½]". Bind off.

## Left Front

Cast on 51 (57, 63) [39, 45, 51] stitches. *Begin Chart Pattern: Row 1* (RS) K1, then beginning as indicated for left front, work chart pattern to last stitch, ending as indicated, k1. Continue in pattern as established until piece measures same length as back to underarm, end with a WS row.
*Shape armhole*
Shape armhole at beginning of RS rows as for back—40 (46, 52) [32, 38, 44] stitches. Work even until armhole measures 5 (6, 6½) [4½, 5, 5½]", end with a RS row.
*Shape neck*
*Next row* (WS) Bind off 10 (11, 13) [9, 11, 13] stitches (neck edge), work to end. Decrease 1 stitch at neck edge every row 7 [5] times, then every other row 3 (4, 4) [2] times—20 (24, 28) [16, 20, 24] stitches. Work even until armhole measures same length as back to shoulders. Bind off.

## Right Front

Cast on 51 (57, 63) [39, 45, 51] stitches. *Begin Chart Pattern: Row 1* (RS) K1, then beginning as indicated for right front, work chart pattern to last stitch, ending as indicated, k1. Complete to correspond to left front, reversing armhole and neck shaping.

## Sleeves

Cast on 51 [39] stitches. *Begin Chart Pattern: Row 1* (RS) K1, then beginning as indicated for sleeve, work chart pattern to last stitch, ending as indicated, k1. Continue in pattern as established, AT SAME TIME, increase 1 stitch each side (working increases inside selvage stitches and into pattern) every 8th [8th, 8th, 6th] row 5 (10, 20) [5, 10, 3] times, then every 10th [10th, 10th, 8th] row 11 (8, 1) [6, 2, 11] times—83 (87, 93) [61, 63, 67] stitches. Work even until piece measures 16 (17, 18) [17, 17, 18]" from beginning, end with a WS row.
*Shape cap*
Bind off 5 [4] stitches at beginning of next 2 rows. *Decrease row* (RS) K2, SSK, work in pattern to last 4 stitches, k2tog, k2. Repeat decrease row every other row 5 [2] times more. Work 3 rows even. Bind off remaining 61 (65, 71) [47, 49, 53] stitches.

## Finishing

Block pieces. Sew shoulders.
*Neck edging*
With RS facing, beginning at right front neck edge, pick up and knit 38 (40, 42) [23, 25, 27] stitches to shoulder, 37 (41, 45) [29, 33, 37] stitches along back neck, 38 (40, 42) [23, 25, 27] stitches along left front neck—113 (121, 129) [75, 83, 91] stitches. Knit 3 rows. *Make buttonloop: Next row* (RS) Cast on 16 [12] stitches, then bind off all stitches knitwise, including cast-on stitches.
*Front edgings*
With RS facing, pick up and knit 83 (93, 99) [58, 63, 67] stitches evenly along front edge. Knit 1 row. Bind off all stitches knitwise. Sew end of buttonloop to front edge about ¾" down from neck edge.
*Armhole edgings* (for vest version only)
With RS facing, pick up and knit stitches evenly around armhole. Knit 1 row. Bind off knitwise.
Sew on button. Set in sleeves. Sew side and sleeve seams.

**yarn**
Version 1 (as shown on page 42) BERROCO Ultra Silk (rayon; nylon; silk; 50g; 98 yds) Frond
Version 2 (as shown above) CLASSIC ELITE Sand (cotton; 50g; 127 yds) Teal
Version 2 (as shown on page 43 and 45) REYNOLDS Ole' Ole' (cotton; acrylic; 50g; 80 yds) Jade Green

### Split Leaf Chart

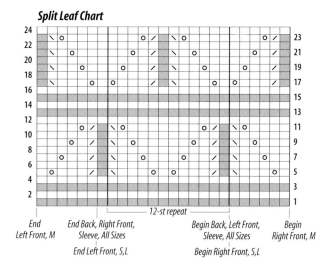

End Left Front, M | End Back, Right Front, Sleeve, All Sizes | End Left Front, S,L | 12-st repeat | Begin Back, Left Front, Sleeve, All Sizes | Begin Right Front, S,L | Begin Right Front, M

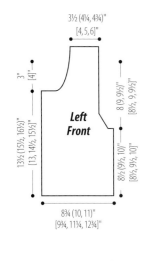

3½ (4¼, 4¾)"
[4, 5, 6]"

3" [4]"

8 (9, 9½)"
[8½, 9, 9½]"

13½ (15½, 16½)"
[13, 14½, 15½]"

**Left Front**

8½ (9½, 10)"
[8½, 9½, 10]"

8¾ (10, 11)"
[9¾, 11¼, 12¾]"

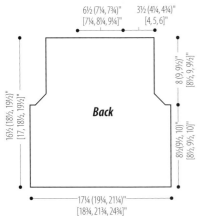

6½ (7¼, 7¾)"
[7¼, 8¼, 9¼]"

3½ (4¼, 4¾)"
[4, 5, 6]"

8 (9, 9½)"
[8½, 9, 9½]

16½ (18½, 19½)"
[17, 18½, 19½]"

**Back**

8½ (9½, 10)"
[8½, 9½, 10]"

17¼ (19¼, 21¼)"
[18¾, 21¾, 24¾]"

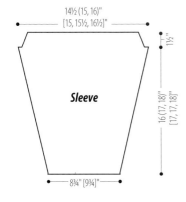

14½ (15, 16)"
[15, 15½, 16½]"

1½"

**Sleeve**

16 (17, 18)"
[17, 17, 18]"

8¾" [9¾]"

**Stitch key**
- ☐ Knit on RS, purl on WS
- ▧ Purl on RS, knit on WS
- ⊙ Yarn over
- ⁄ K2tog
- ⟍ SSK

# half-linen to gold

it's easy
...go for it!

**EASY +**

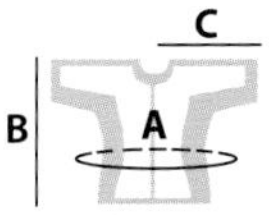

C

B | A

**LOOSE FIT**

**Sizes S (M, L)**
**Shown in Small**
A 38¼ (44¼, 50¼)"
B 16¾ (18, 19½)"
C 26 (27½, 30)"

**10cm/4"**
26
16
• over half-linen stitch

1 2 3 **4** 5 6

• Medium weight
735 (860, 1000) yds

• 5mm/US 8, or size to obtain gauge

• one 25mm/1"

**yarn**
FIESTA Insignia La
Boheme (mohair; rayon;
nylon; 114g; 165 yds)
Bandalier

**Half-linen stitch** (multiple of 2 + 1)
*Row 1* (RS) * K1, sl 1 purlwise with yarn in front (sl 1 wyif); repeat from *, end k1.
*Rows 2 and 4* Purl.
*Row 3* K2, * sl 1 wyif, k1; repeat from *, end k1.
Repeat rows 1–4 for half-linen stitch.

## Back

Cast on 75 (87, 99) stitches. Knit 3 rows. Work in half-linen stitch until piece measures 9½ (9½, 10)" from beginning, end with a WS row.
*Shape armholes*
Bind off 4 stitches at beginning of next 2 rows. Work 2 rows even. Decrease 1 stitch each side on next row, then every other row 2 times more—61 (73, 85) stitches. Work even until armhole measures 7¼ (8½, 9½)". Bind off.

## Left Front

Cast on 39 (45, 51) stitches. Knit 3 rows. Work in half-linen stitch until piece measures same length as back to underarm, end with a WS row.
*Shape armhole*
Shape armhole at beginning of RS rows as for back—32 (38, 44) stitches. Work even until armhole measures 3¾ (5, 6)", end with a RS row.
*Shape neck*
*Next row* (WS) Bind off 9 (11, 13) stitches (neck edge), work to end. Decrease 1 stitch at neck edge every row 5 times, then every other row twice—16 (20, 24) stitches. Work even until armhole measures same length as back to shoulders. Bind off.

## Right Front

Work as for left front, reversing shaping.

## Sleeves

Cast on 39 stitches. Knit 3 rows. Work in half-linen stitch, AT SAME TIME, keeping first and last stitch in stockinette stitch (knit on RS, purl on WS), increase 1 stitch each side (working increases into pattern) every 10th (8th, 8th) row 3 (4, 11) times, then every 12th (10th, 10th) row 6 (7, 2) times—57 (61, 65) stitches. Work even until piece measures 17 (17, 18)" from beginning, end with a WS row.
*Shape cap*
Bind off 4 stitches at beginning of next 2 rows. Decrease 1 stitch each side on next row, then every other row 2 times more.
Work 3 rows even. Bind off remaining 43 (47, 51) stitches.

## Finishing

Block pieces. Sew shoulders.
*Neck edging*
With RS facing, beginning at right front neck edge, pick up and knit 23 (25, 27) stitches to shoulder, 29 (33, 37) stitches along back neck, and 23 (25, 27) stitches along left front neck—75 (83, 91) stitches. Knit 3 rows. *Make buttonloop: Next row* (RS) Cast on 12 stitches, then bind off all stitches knitwise, including cast-on stitches.
*Front edgings*
With RS facing, pick up and knit 65 (67, 69) stitches evenly along front edge. Knit 1 row. Bind off all stitches knitwise. Sew end of buttonloop to front edge about ¾" down from neck edge. Sew on button. Set in sleeves. Sew side and sleeve seams.

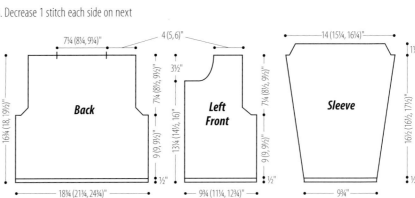

7¼ (8¼, 9¼)"    4 (5, 6)"    14 (15¼, 16¼)"

**Back**    **Left Front**    **Sleeve**

16¾ (18, 19½)"    7¼ (8½, 9½)"    3½"    7¼ (8½, 9½)"    1½"    16½ (16½, 17½)"

9 (9, 9½)"    13¼ (14½, 16)"    9 (9, 9½)"

½"    ½"    ½"

18¾ (21¾, 24¾)"    9¾ (11¼, 12¾)"    9¾"

Jean Frost

*The age-old feather and fan stitch of afghan-making fame takes on a new life in a cardigan worked in one piece to the armhole. You'll wear it often from spring to fall!*

# deep purple days

## INTERMEDIATE

**STANDARD FIT**

**Sizes S (M, L, 1X)**
**Shown in Medium**
A 37¾ (42, 48, 54)"
B 20½ (21½, 22½, 23½)"
C 28 (29½, 31, 32½)"

**10cm/4"**
26
21
**• over chart pattern**

1 2 3 4 **5** 6

• **Bulky weight**
• 1335 (1505, 1710, 1935) yds

• 3.75mm/US 5, *or size to obtain gauge*, 90cm/36" long

## &

• stitch holders

*original yarn*

SCHOELLER ESSLINGER/SKACEL
Palmeros (cotton blend; 50g;
98 yds) purple
Reknit (as shown on pages
49 and 50) LOUISA HARDING
Kashmir Aran (wool;
microfiber; cashmere; 50g;
83 yds) dark teal

## Notes

**1** See *School*, page 94, for 3-needle bind-off. **2** Body is worked in one piece to underarm; then fronts and back are worked separately to shoulder. **3** Keep 1 stitch at each edge in garter stitch (knit every row) for selvage stitches. **4** When working shaping, if there are not enough stitches to work a yarn over with its corresponding decrease, work stitches in stockinette stitch.

## Body

Cast on 195 (227, 259, 291) stitches. ***Work reverse stockinette stitch (rev st st) band: Rows 1, 3 and 5*** (RS) K1 (selvage), purl to last stitch, k1 (selvage). ***Rows 2 and 4*** Knit. ***Begin Chart Pattern: Rows 1, 2 and 3*** Knit. ***Row 4*** (RS) K1 (selvage), then beginning as indicated for body, work chart pattern to last stitch, ending as indicated for body, k1. Continue in chart pattern as established until piece measures 12½ (13, 13½, 14)" from beginning, end with a RS row.

*Divide for fronts and back*

***Next row*** (WS) Work 49 (57, 65, 73) stitches and place them on hold for left front, work 97 (113, 129, 145) stitches and place them on hold for back, work remaining 49 (57, 65, 73) stitches for right front.

## Right Front

***Next row*** (RS) Work in pattern to end, cast on 1 stitch for selvage—50 (58, 66, 74) stitches. Work even until armhole measures 6 (6½, 7, 7½)", end with a WS row.

*Shape neck*

***Next row*** (RS) Bind off 10 stitches (neck edge), work to end. Decrease 1 stitch at neck edge every row 12 times—28 (36, 44, 52) stitches. When armhole measures 8 (8½, 9, 9½)", place stitches on hold.

## Left Front

***Next row*** (RS) Join yarn at armhole edge, cast on 1 stitch for selvage, work to end—50 (58, 66, 74) stitches. Work to correspond to right front, reversing neck shaping.

## Back

***Next row*** (RS) Join yarn at armhole edge, cast on 1 stitch for selvage, work to end, cast on 1 stitch for selvage—99 (115, 131, 147) stitches. Work even until armhole measures same length as fronts to shoulders. Place stitches on hold.

## Sleeves

Cast on 51 stitches. Work 5-row rev st st band as for body. ***Begin Chart Pattern: Rows 1, 2 and 3*** Knit. ***Row 4*** (RS) K1, then beginning as indicated for sleeve, work chart pattern to last stitch, k1. Continue in pattern as established, AT SAME TIME, increase 1 stitch each side (working increase stitches into pattern), on next row, then every 6th (4th, 4th, 4th) row 11 (1, 10, 16) times, then every 8th (6th, 6th, 6th) row 5 (17, 11, 7) times—85 (89, 95, 99) stitches. Work even until piece measures 18½" from beginning. Bind off.

## Finishing

Block pieces. Join shoulders, using 3-needle bind-off, as follows: join 28 (36, 44, 52) stitches of first shoulder, bind off back neck stitches until 28 (36, 44, 52) stitches remain, join 2nd shoulder. With RS facing, pick up and knit 85 (91, 95, 99) stitches evenly around armhole. With RS together, join sleeve to body with 3-needle bind-off.

*Front and neck edging*

With RS facing, begin above rev st st band and pick up and knit 74 (78, 82, 86) stitches along right front, 20 stitches along right front neck, k43 stitches along back neck (decrease to 34 stitches), 20 stitches along left front neck, and 74 (78, 82, 86) stitches along left front to rev st st band—222 (230, 238, 246) stitches. Work 5 rows in rev st st. Bind off loosely. Tack edges of front bands to lower edge bands.

16 (17, 18, 19)"

**Sleeve**

18"

9¾"

½"

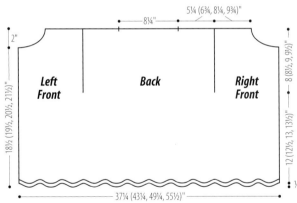

5¼ (6¾, 8¼, 9¾)"

8¼"

2"

18½ (19½, 20½, 21½)"

**Left Front**

**Back**

**Right Front**

12 (12½, 13, 13½)"

8 (8½, 9, 9½)"

½"

37¼ (43¼, 49¼, 55½)"

**Chart pattern**

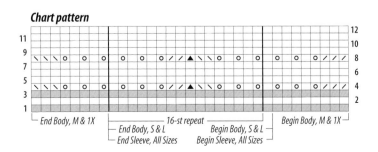

11   9   7   5   3   1

12   10   8   6   4   2

End Body, M & 1X

End Body, S & L
End Sleeve, All Sizes

16-st repeat

Begin Body, S & L
Begin Sleeve, All Sizes

Begin Body, M & 1X

**Stitch key**

☐ Knit on RS, purl on WS

▨ Purl on RS, knit on WS

╲ SSK

╱ K2tog

⊙ Yarn over

▲ S2KP2

Use this versatile, fun-to-knit cardigan as a replacement for your work-day requirements, and you'll leave the traditional tailored suit jacket far behind.

Jean Frost

# bobbly-pointed edges

**INTERMEDIATE**

**STANDARD FIT**

**Sizes S (M, L)**
**Shown in Small**
A 39 (41, 45)"
B 18 (20¼, 24)"
C 30 (31½, 33½)"

12.5 (13, 14.5)cm/5 (5¼, 5¾)"

**34**

9.5 (10, 11.5)cm/3¾ (4, 4½)"

**24**

**• over Chart Pattern,**
**using 3.5mm/US 4, (4mm/US 6,**
**5mm/US 8) needles**

1 2 3  5 6

**• Medium weight**
1075 (1225, 1600) yds

3.5mm/US 4 (4mm/US 6,
5mm/ US 8), or size to obtain
gauge

3.5mm/US 4 (4mm/US 6,
5mm/ US 8), or size to obtain
gauge 74cm/29" long

**• cable needle (cn)**
**• stitch holders**
**• stitch markers**

## Notes

**1** See *School*, page 94, for SSK, SSP, yarn over (yo) before a knit and purl stitch, and 3-needle bind-off. **2** Size differences occur by changing needle sizes rather than stitch numbers. **3** To maintain correct stitch count when shaping, every decrease in chart pattern needs a corresponding yo. **4** Keep first and last stitch in reverse stockinette stitch (purl on RS, knit on WS) for selvage.

## Make Bobble (MB)

*On a RS row* Knit into front, back, front, back of stitch, [turn, p4, turn, k4] 3 times; pass 2nd, 3rd and 4th stitches, one at a time, over first stitch and off needle.
*On a WS row* Purl into front, back, front, back of stitch, [turn, k4, turn, p4] 3 times; complete as for RS bobble.

## Decrease Rows

*At beginning of a RS row* P1, k2tog.
*At end of a RS row* SSK, p1.
*At beginning of a WS row* K1, SSP.
*At end of a WS row* P2tog, k1.

## Back

With size 4 (6, 8) needles, cast on 137 stitches. Knit 1 row.
*Bobble row* (RS) K8, * MB, k8, p1, k7; repeat from * to last 10 stitches, MB, k9. Work 6 rows of chart pattern 10 (11, 12) times, then work rows 1–5 once more. Piece measures approximately 10½ (12¼, 14¾)" from beginning.
*Shape armholes*
Bind off 9 stitches at beginning of next 2 rows. Decrease 1 stitch each side on next row, then every other row 6 times more—105 stitches. *Next row* (WS) K1, work 17-stitch repeat of chart row 3 to last stitch, end k1. Work even until armhole measures approximately 7½ (8, 9¼)", end with chart row 6. Place stitches on hold.

## Right Front

With size 4 (6, 8) needles, cast on 69 stitches. Work as for back until piece measures same length as back to underarm, end with chart row 6. Shape armhole by binding off 9 stitches at beginning of next WS row, then decreasing 1 stitch at end of every RS row 7 times—53 stitches. Work even until armhole measures approximately 3¾ (4, 4¾)", end with chart row 1.

*original yarn*

BROWN SHEEP Nature Spun Worsted (wool; 100g; 245 yds) Blue

*Shape neck*
*Next row* (RS) Bind off 9 stitches (neck edge), work to end. Decrease 1 stitch at beginning of every RS row 7 times—37 stitches. Work even until armhole measures same length as back to shoulder. Place stitches on hold.

## Left Front

Work to correspond to right front, reversing shaping. Begin armhole shaping after chart row 5 and shape armhole at beginning of RS rows. Begin neck shaping after chart row 6 and bind off 9 stitches at beginning of next WS row. Decrease 1 stitch at end of every RS row 7 times.

## Sleeves

With size 4 (6, 8) needles, cast on 69 stitches. Work as for back until 6 rows of chart pattern have been worked 8 (7, 6) times, then work rows 1–5 once more. Piece measures approximately 8½ (8¼, 8)" from beginning. Continue in chart pattern, AT SAME TIME, increase 1 stitch each side (working increases into pattern) on next row, then every 6th row 8 times more—87 stitches. Work 5 rows even. Piece measures approximately 17 (17¼, 18)" from beginning.
*Shape cap*
Bind off 9 stitches at beginning of next 2 rows. Decrease 1 stitch each side on next row, then every other row 9 times more, then every row 13 times. Bind off 5 stitches at beginning of next 2 rows. Bind off remaining 13 stitches.

## Finishing

Block pieces. Join shoulders, using 3-needle bind-off, as follows: Join 37 stitches of first shoulder, bind off back neck stitches until 37 stitches remain, join 2nd shoulder.
*Front edging*
With RS facing and size 4 (6, 8) circular needle, pick up and knit 84 (90, 96) stitches along right front edge to neck, 3 stitches in corner stitch, 34 stitches to shoulder, 31 stitches along back neck, 34 stitches along left front neck, 3 stitches in corner stitch, and 84 (90, 96) stitches along left front edge—273 (285, 297) stitches. *Bobble row* (WS) K6 (12, 0), MB in next stitch, [k17, MB] 4 (4, 5) times, k5. (**Note** Bobbles along left front edge serve as buttons and yo's of chart row 1 on right front edge as buttonholes.) Bind off all stitches knitwise. Set in sleeves. Sew side and sleeve seams.

**Chart Pattern**

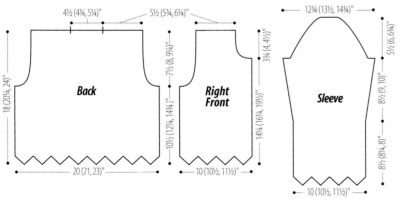

17-st repeat

**Back**

18 (20¼, 24)"
20 (21, 23)"
4½ (4¾, 5¼)"
5½ (5¾, 6¼)"
7½ (8, 9¼)"
10½ (12¼, 14¾)"

**Right Front**

10 (10½, 11½)"
14¼ (16¾, 19½)"

**Sleeve**

12¾ (13½, 14¾)"
3¾ (4, 4½)"
5½ (6, 6¾)"
8½ (9, 10)"
8½ (8¾, 8)"
10 (10½, 11½)"

**Stitch key**

☐ Knit on RS, purl on WS

▨ Purl on RS, knit on WS

⊙ Yarn over

╱ K2tog on RS, p2tog on WS

╲ SSK on RS, SSP on WS

⧗ **1/3 LC** *Sl 2 to cn, hold to front, k2; sl last st from cn to LH needle and k it; k1 from cn.*

## ADVANCED

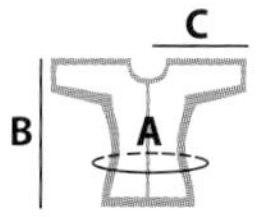

**STANDARD FIT**
**Sizes S (M, L, 1X, 2X)**
**Shown in Medium**
JACKET **A** 37¼ (41, 46¼, 50, 54¼)"
**B** 23 (23, 23½, 23½, 24)"
**C** 24 (24½, 25, 26, 27)"

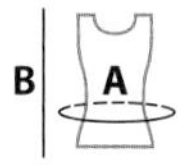

**VERY CLOSE FIT**
**Sizes S (M, L, 1X, 2X)**
**Shown in Medium**
SHELL **A** 32½ (37, 41½, 46, 51)"
**B** 19 (19, 19½, 19½, 20)"

**10cm/4"**

*30 /40*

*18/22*
JACKET/SHELL • **over garter stitch (knit every row)**

1 2 3 **4** 5 6

• **Medium weight**
JACKET • 1040 (1120, 1235, 1320, 1435) yds
SHELL • 730 (830, 955, 1060, 1200) yds

JACKET • 4mm/US 6, *or size to obtain gauge*
SHELL • 3.5mm/US 4, *or size to obtain gauge*

JACKET • two 4mm/US 6
SHELL • two 3.5mm/US 4

JACKET • five 20mm/¾"

• cable needle (cn)
• stitch holders and markers

*original yarn*

*Cabling, I-cords and garter stitch create a wonderful new-looking tailored jacket and shell. The yarns are blends of wool and cotton mixed with angora and silk for all-season wearing.*

# two blue

### Notes

**1** See *School*, page 94, for SSK, Make 1 (M1) purl, invisible cast-on, cable cast-on, I-cord, grafting and short-rows. **2** Slip (sl) stitches purlwise with yarn at WS of work. **3** Use invisible cast-on for all I-cords and cable cast-on for all other cast-ons. **4** Sl 1 stitch at beginning and end of WS rows until underarm, then work these stitches in stockinette stitch (St st) (knit on RS, purl on WS). **5** Work selvage stitch at center front edge of jacket in St st.

### DECREASE ROWS

*At beginning of RS rows* K2, k2tog.
*At end of RS rows* SSK, k2.

### INCREASE ROWS

*At beginning of RS rows* K1, knit into front and back of 2nd stitch (kf&b).
*At end of RS rows* Kf&b in 3rd stitch from end, k2.

### I-CORD SHORT ROWS

*Row 1* K3, sl 1, do not turn, slide stitches to opposite end of needle. *Row 2* K2, sl 2, slide stitches. *Row 3* K4, slide stitches. *Rows 4–6* Repeat Rows 1–3.

### 3/3 RIGHT CABLE (RC)

Sl 3 to cn, hold to back, k3; k3 from cn.

### 3/3 LEFT CABLE (LC)

Sl 3 to cn, hold to front, k3; k3 from cn.

### SHELL
### Back

With double-pointed needles (dpn), invisibly cast on 4 stitches. Work I-cord for 88 (100, 112, 124, 138) rows. Place stitches on hold. With straight needles, cast on 1 stitch, then pick up and knit 88 (100, 112, 124, 138) stitches in cord, cast on 1 stitch—90 (102, 114, 126, 140) stitches. Work in garter stitch for 115 rows. Piece measures approximately 12" from beginning.
*Shape armholes*
Bind off 5 (6, 7, 7, 7) stitches at beginning of next 2 rows, 4 stitches at beginning of next 0 (0, 0, 2, 2) rows, 3 stitches at beginning of next 0 (0, 2, 2, 4) rows, 2 stitches

at beginning of next 2 (6, 6, 4, 6) rows. Decrease 1 stitch each side every RS row 7 (5, 4, 5, 3) times—62 (68, 74, 80, 88) stitches. Work 35 (35, 41, 39, 43) rows even. Armhole measures approximately 5¼ (5¼, 5¾, 5¾, 6¼)".
*Shape neck*
*Next row* (RS) K18 (19, 21, 22, 24), join 2nd ball of yarn and bind off next 26 (30, 32, 36, 40) stitches, knit to end. Working both sides at same time, decrease 1 stitch at each neck edge every RS row 6 times—12 (13, 15, 16, 18) stitches each side. Work 5 rows even. Armhole measures approximately 7 (7, 7½, 7½, 8)". Bind off all stitches.

### Front

*Lower right piece*
With dpn, invisibly cast on 4 stitches and work I-cord for 36 (42, 48, 54, 61) rows. Work 6 I-cord short rows. With straight needles, k4 cord stitches, skip 1 row, then pick up and knit 37 (43, 49, 55, 62) stitches along I-cord, cast on 1 stitch—42 (48, 54, 60, 67) stitches. *Rows 1 and 3* (WS) Sl 1, knit to last 4 stitches, sl 4. *Row 2* Knit. *Row 4* K4, kf&b, knit to end. Repeat last 4 rows 4 times more, then work Row 1 once—47 (53, 59, 65, 72) stitches. Place stitches on hold. Cut yarn.
*Lower left piece*
With dpn, invisibly cast on 4 stitches and work 6 I-cord short rows, then work I-cord for 36 (42, 48, 54, 61) rows. Place stitches on hold. With straight needles, cast on 1 stitch, then beginning at end of cord where stitches are on hold, pick up and knit 37 (43, 49, 55, 62) stitches along I-cord, place 4 stitches from cord cast-on onto dpn (removing waste yarn), then knit these 4 stitches onto straight needle—42 (48, 54, 60, 67) stitches. *Rows 1 and 3* (WS) Sl 4, knit to last stitch, sl 1. *Row 2* Knit. *Row 4* Knit to last 5 stitches, kf&b, k4. Repeat last 4 rows 4 times more, then work Row 1 once—47 (53, 59, 65, 72) stitches.
*Join pieces*
*Next row* (RS) Knit to last 4 stitches of left piece, sl 4 stitches to cn, hold to front, place stitches of right piece onto left needle ready to work a RS row and k2tog, k2; [k2, k2tog] from cn, knit to end—92 (104, 116, 128, 142) stitches. *Begin Cable Pattern: Rows 1, 3 and 5* (WS) Sl 1, k42 (48, 54, 60, 67), p6, k42 (48, 54, 60, 67), sl 1. *Rows 2 and 4* Knit. *Row 6* K43 (49, 55, 61, 68), 3/3 LC, k43 (49, 55, 61, 68). Repeat Rows 1-6 until piece measures same length as back to underarm.
*Shape armholes*
Shape armholes as for back—64 (70, 76, 82, 90) stitches. Work 16 (16, 16, 14, 14) rows even, ending with a cable row. Armhole measures approximately 3¼".

JACKET PLYMOUTH/CLECKHEATON'S Nature Angora/Silk 8-Ply (angora, silk, wool, nylon; 25g; 70 yds) powder blue
SHELL PLYMOUTH/CLECKHEATON'S Nature Cotton/Wool 8-Ply (cotton, wool; 50g; 138 yds) medium blue

## Shape neck

**Next row** (WS) Work 29 (32, 35, 38, 42) stitches, p2, M1 purl, p1, join a 2nd ball of yarn and p1, M1 purl, p2, work to end—33 (36, 39, 42, 46) stitches each side. Working both sides at same time, work as follows: **Row 1** (RS) Knit to 7 stitches before neck edge, k2tog, k5; on 2nd side, k5, SSK, knit to end. **Rows 2 and 4** P1, knit to 4 stitches before neck edge, sl 4; on 2nd side, sl 4, knit to last stitch, p1. **Row 3** Knit. Repeat last 4 rows 3 times more, then work rows 1–3 once—28 (31, 34, 37, 41) stitches each side.

## Continue neck shaping

**Next row** (WS) Work to 4 stitches before neck edge, place 4 stitches on hold; on 2nd side, place first 4 stitches on hold, then bind off next 4 (5, 4, 5, 5) stitches, work to end. **Next row** Work to end of first side; on 2nd side, bind off 4 (5, 4, 5, 5) stitches, work to end. Continue to bind off from each neck edge 2 (3, 2, 3, 3) stitches once, then decrease 1 stitch at each neck edge every RS row 6 (6, 9, 9, 11) times—12 (13, 15, 16, 18) stitches each side. Work 1 row even. Bind off.

## Finishing

Block pieces. Sew shoulders. Sew side seams, grafting I-cord edges together.

### Neck I-Cord trim

With RS facing, begin at right front neck and place 4 cord stitches on dpn. Work 6 I-cord short rows, * pick up and knit 1 stitch from neck edge (5 stitches on needle), slide stitches to opposite end of needle, k3, k2tog throught back loops (tbl); repeat from * around neck edge to left front neck, work 6 I-cord short rows, then graft I-cord ends together.

### Armhole I-Cord trim

With dpn, invisibly cast on 4 stitches. With RS facing, begin at side seam and * pick up and knit 1 stitch from armhole edge, slide stitches to opposite end of needle, k3, k2tog tbl; repeat from * around armhole. Graft ends together.

→ Direction of knitting I-cord

## JACKET

### Back

*Lower left piece*

With dpn, invisibly cast on 4 stitches and work I-cord for 33 (38, 43, 47, 52) rows. Work 6 I-cord short rows. With straight needles, k4 cord stitches, skip 1 row, then pick up and knit 34 (39, 44, 48, 53) stitches along I-cord, cast on 1 stitch—39 (44, 49, 53, 58) stitches. **Rows 1 and 3** (WS) Sl 1, knit to last 4 stitches, sl 4. **Row 2** Knit. **Row 4** K4, kf&b, knit to end. Repeat last 4 rows 3 times more, then work row 1 once more—43 (48, 53, 57, 62) stitches. Place stitches on hold. Cut yarn.

*Lower right piece*

With dpn, invisibly cast on 4 stitches and work 6 I-cord short rows, then work I-cord for 33 (38, 43, 47, 52) rows. Place stitches on hold. With straight needles, beginning at end of cord where stitches are on hold, cast on 1 stitch, then pick up and knit 34 (39, 44, 48, 53) stitches along I-cord, place 4 stitches from cord cast-on onto dpn (removing waste yarn), then knit these 4 stitches onto straight needle—39 (44, 49, 53, 58) stitches. *Rows 1 and 3* (WS) Sl 4, knit to last stitch, sl 1. *Row 2* Knit. *Row 4* Knit to last 5 stitches, kf&b, k4. Repeat last 4 rows 3 times more, then work row 1 once more—43 (48, 53, 57, 62) stitches.

*Join pieces*

*Next row* (RS) Knit to last 4 stitches of right piece, sl 4 stitches to cn, hold to back, place stitches of left piece onto left needle ready to work a RS row and k2tog, k2; [k2, k2tog] from cn, knit to end—84 (94, 104, 112, 122) stitches. *Begin Cable Pattern: Rows 1, 3 and 5* (WS) Sl 1, k38 (43, 48, 52, 57), p6, k38 (43, 48, 52, 57), sl 1. *Rows 2 and 4* Knit. *Row 6* K39 (44, 49, 53, 58), 3/3 RC, k39 (44, 49, 53, 58).

*Shape waist*

Continue in pattern as established, working 3/3 RC over center 6 stitches every 6th row, AT SAME TIME, decrease 1 stitch each side on next RS row, then every 6th row 4 times more—74 (84, 94, 102, 112) stitches. Work 5 rows even. Increase 1 stitch each side on next row, then every 6th row 4 times more—84 (94, 104, 112, 122) stitches. Work even until piece measures 14" from beginning, end with a WS row.

*Shape armholes*

Bind off 4 (5, 6, 6, 6) stitches at beginning of next 2 rows, 4 stitches at beginning of next 0 (0, 0, 0, 2) rows. Decrease 1 stitch each side on next row, then every other row 1 (3, 4, 6, 6) times more, then every 4th row once—70 (74, 80, 84, 86) stitches. Work even until armhole measures 8 (8, 8½, 8½, 9)", end with a WS row.

*Shape shoulders*

Bind off 5 stitches at beginning of next 2 (6, 10, 8, 8) rows, 4 (4, 0, 6, 6) stitches at beginning of next 8 (4, 0, 2, 2) rows. Bind off remaining 28 (28, 30, 32, 34) stitches.

**Right Front**

*Lower right piece*

With dpn, invisibly cast on 4 stitches and work I-cord for 13 (16, 21, 25, 29) rows. Work 6 I-cord short rows. With straight needles, k4 cord stitches, skip 1 row, then pick up and knit 14 (17, 22, 26, 30) stitches along I-cord, cast on 1 stitch—19 (22, 27, 31, 35) stitches. *Rows 1 and 3* (WS) Sl 1, knit to last 4 stitches, sl 4. *Row 2* Knit. *Row 4* K4, kf&b, knit to end. Repeat last 4 rows 3 times more, then work row 1 once more—23 (26, 31, 35, 39) stitches. Place stitches on hold. Cut yarn.

*Lower left piece*

With dpn, invisibly cast on 4 stitches and work 6 I-cord short rows, then work I-cord for 13 (14, 15, 16, 17) rows. Place stitches on hold. With straight needles, beginning at end of cord where stitches are on hold, cast on 1 stitch, then pick up and knit 14 (15, 16, 17, 18) stitches along I-cord, place 4 stitches from cord cast-on onto dpn (removing waste yarn), then knit these 4 stitches onto straight needle—19 (20, 21, 22, 23) stitches. *Rows 1 and 3* (WS) Sl 4, knit to last stitch, p 1. *Row 2* Knit. *Row 4* Knit to last 5 stitches, kf&b, k4. Repeat last 4 rows 3 times more, then work row 1 once more—23 (24, 25, 26, 27) stitches.

*Join pieces*

*Next row* (RS) Knit to last 4 stitches of left piece, sl 4 stitches to cn, hold to front, place stitches of right piece onto left needle ready to work a RS row and k2tog, k2; [k2, k2tog] from cn, knit to end—44 (48, 54, 59, 64) stitches. *Begin Cable Pattern: Rows 1, 3 and 5* (WS) Sl 1, k18 (21, 26, 30, 34), p6, k18 (19, 20, 21, 22), p1. *Rows 2 and 4* Knit. *Row 6* K19 (20, 21, 22, 23), 3/3 LC, k19 (22, 27, 31, 35). Continue as for back, shaping waist and armhole at side edge only—37 (38, 42, 45, 46) stitches. Work even until piece measures 19¼ (19¼, 19¾, 19¾, 20¼)" from beginning, end with a WS row.

*Shape lapel notch*

*Next row* (RS) Bind off 13 (14, 15, 16, 17) stitches, work to end. *Next row* Work to end, then cast on 13 (14, 15, 16, 17) stitches over bound-off stitches. Work even until piece measures same length as back to shoulder. Shape shoulder at beginning of WS rows as for back—16 (15, 17, 19, 20) stitches.

*Shape collar*

**Note:** Do not hide short-row wraps.

*Next row* (RS) K3, wrap next stitch and turn (W&T), work to end. *Next row* Work 5 stitches, W&T, work to end. *Next row* Work 7 stitches, W&T, work to end. Work 4 (4, 6, 6, 6) rows more, working 2 additional stitches on every RS row. *Next row* (RS) K11 (11, 13 13, 13), W&T, work to end. Working 2 fewer stitches on each RS row, work 8 (8, 10, 10, 10) more rows. Work even for 2¾ (2¾, 3, 3¼, 3½)", end with a WS row. *Next row* K9 (9, 9, 12, 12) stitches, W&T, work to end. Work 4 (4, 4, 6, 6) more rows, working 3 fewer stitches on each RS row. *Next row* (RS) Work across all stitches. Place stitches on hold.

**Left Front**

*Lower right piece*

With dpn, invisibly cast on 4 stitches and work I-cord for 13 (14, 15, 16, 17) rows. Work 6 I-cord short rows. With straight needles, k4 cord stitches, skip 1 row, then pick up and knit 14 (15, 16, 17, 18) stitches along I-cord, cast on 1 stitch—19 (20, 21, 22, 23) stitches. *Rows 1 and 3* (WS) P1, knit to last 4 stitches, sl 4. *Row 2* Knit. *Row 4* K4, kf&b, knit to end. Repeat last 4 rows 3 times more, then work row 1 once more—23 (24, 25, 26, 27) stitches. Place stitches on hold. Cut yarn.

*Lower left piece*

With dpn, invisibly cast on 4 stitches and work 6 I-cord short rows, then work I-cord for 13 (16, 21, 25, 29) rows. Place stitches on hold. With straight needles, beginning at end of cord where stitches are on hold, cast on 1 stitch, then pick up and knit 14 (17, 22, 26, 30) stitches along I-cord, place 4 stitches from cord cast-on onto dpn (removing waste yarn), then knit these 4 stitches onto straight needle—19 (22, 27, 31, 35) stitches. *Rows 1 and 3* (WS) Sl 4, knit to last stitch, sl 1. *Row 2* Knit. *Row 4* Knit to last 5 stitches, kf&b, k4. Repeat last 4 rows 3 times more, then work row 1 once more—23 (26, 31, 35, 39) stitches.

*Join pieces*

*Next row* (RS) Knit to last 4 stitches of left piece, sl 4 stitches to cn, hold to back, place stitches of right piece onto left needle ready to work a RS row and k2tog, k2; [k2, k2tog] from cn, knit to end—44 (48, 54, 59, 64) stitches. *Begin Cable Pattern: Rows 1, 3 and 5* P1, k18 (19, 20, 21, 22), p6, k18 (21, 26, 30, 34), sl 1. *Rows 2 and 4* Knit. *Row 6* K19 (22, 27, 31, 35), 3/3 RC, k19 (20, 21, 22, 23). Complete to correspond to right front, reversing shaping. Bind off for lapel notch at beginning of a WS row. Reverse collar shaping by working short rows on WS rows. Hide short-row wraps.

**Right Sleeve**

*Lower right piece*

With dpn, invisibly cast on 4 stitches and work I-cord for 16 (18, 19, 20, 21) rows. Work 6 I-cord short rows. With straight needles, k4 cord stitches, skip 1 row, then pick up and knit 17 (19, 20, 21, 22) stitches along I-cord, cast on 1 stitch—22 (24, 25, 26, 27) stitches. *Rows 1 and 3* (WS) Sl 1, knit to last 4 stitches, sl 4. *Row 2* Knit. *Row 4* K4, kf&b, knit to end. Repeat last 4 rows 3 times more, then work row 1 once more—26 (28, 29, 30, 31) stitches. Place stitches on hold. Cut yarn.

*Lower left piece*

With dpn, invisibly cast on 4 stitches and work 6 I-cord short rows, then work I-cord for 16 (18, 19, 20, 21) rows. Place stitches on hold. With straight needles, beginning at end of cord where stitches are on hold, cast on 1 stitch, then pick up and knit 17 (19, 20, 21, 22) stitches along I-cord, place 4 stitches from cord cast-on onto dpn (removing waste yarn), then knit these 4 stitches onto straight needle—22 (24, 25, 26, 27) stitches. *Rows 1 and 3* (WS) Sl 4, knit to last stitch, sl 1. *Row 2* Knit. *Row 4* Knit to last 5 stitches, kf&b, k4. Repeat last 4 rows 3 times more, then work row 1 once more—26 (28, 29, 30, 31) stitches.

*Join pieces*

*Next row* (RS) K1, kf&b, knit to last 4 stitches of left piece, sl 4 stitches to cn, hold to back, place stitches of right piece onto left needle ready to work a RS row and k2tog, k2; [k2, k2tog] from cn, knit to last 2 stitches, kf&b, k1—52 (56, 58, 60, 62) stitches. *Begin Cable Pattern: Row 1* Sl 1, k22 (24, 25, 26, 27), p6, k22 (24, 25, 26, 27), sl 1. Continue in pattern as established, AT SAME TIME, increase 1 stitch each side every 6th row 9 times—70 (74, 76, 78, 80) stitches. Work even until piece measures 11" from beginning, end with a WS row.

*Shape cap*

Bind off 4 (5, 6, 6, 6) stitches at beginning of next 2 rows, 4 stitches at beginning of next 0 (0, 0, 0, 2) rows, 2 stitches at beginning of next 0 (0, 0, 2, 2) rows. ***Size 2X only: Next row*** (RS) Work 4 rows even. Decrease 1 stitch each side on next row, then every 4th row 5 times more. Work 1 row even. ***All Sizes*** Decrease 1 stitch each side on next row, then every other row 16 (16, 19, 18, 5) times more. Work 3 rows even. Bind off 2 (3, 0, 0, 3) stitches at beginning of next 2 (2, 0, 0, 2) rows. Bind off remaining 24 (24, 24, 24, 26) stitches.

**Left Sleeve**

Work to correspond to right sleeve. Join pieces by holding cn to front and working 3/3 LC.

**Finishing**

Block pieces. Sew shoulders. Set in sleeves. Sew side and sleeve seams, grafting I-cord edges together. Graft ends of collar together at center back and sew edge of collar to back neck. Place 5 markers on right front, the first approximately 3 (3, 3½, 3½, 4)" from lower edge, the last approximately 8" above first, and 3 others spaced evenly between.

*Applied I-cord trim*

Sl 4 stitches at lower right front edge to dpn. Work 6 I-cord short-rows. * Pick up and knit 1 stitch from edge—5 stitches. Do not turn. Slide stitches to beginning of dpn and k3, k2tog tbl. Repeat from * along center front, AT SAME TIME, make buttonholes at markers by working 3 unattached I-cord rows. At lapel notch, work 6 I-cord short rows, then continue along notch (bound-off and cast-on stitches), work 6 I-cord short rows, continue around collar, work as before for other notch, then continue along left center front. At lower edge, work I-cord short rows, then graft I-cord ends together at corner. Sew on buttons.

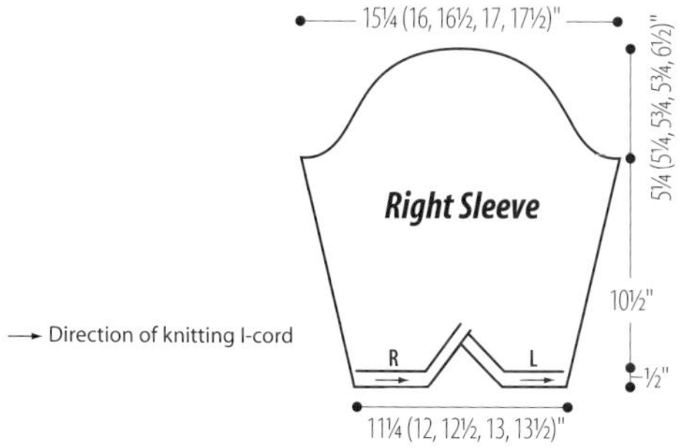

15¼ (16, 16½, 17, 17½)"
5¼ (5¼, 5¾, 5¾, 6½)"
Right Sleeve
10½"
Direction of knitting I-cord
R
L
½"
11¼ (12, 12½, 13, 13½)"


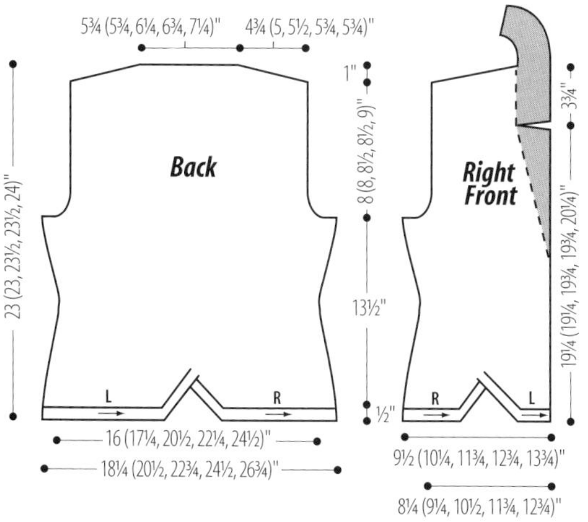

5¾ (5¾, 6¼, 6¾, 7¼)"
4¾ (5, 5½, 5¾, 5¾)"
23 (23, 23½, 23½, 24)"
Back
L
R
16 (17¼, 20½, 22¼, 24½)"
18¼ (20½, 22¾, 24½, 26¾)"
1"
8 (8, 8½, 8½, 9)"
13½"
½"
Right Front
R
L
3¾"
19¼ (19¼, 19¾, 19¾, 20¼)"
9½ (10¼, 11¾, 12¾, 13¾)"
8¼ (9¼, 10½, 11¾, 12¾)"


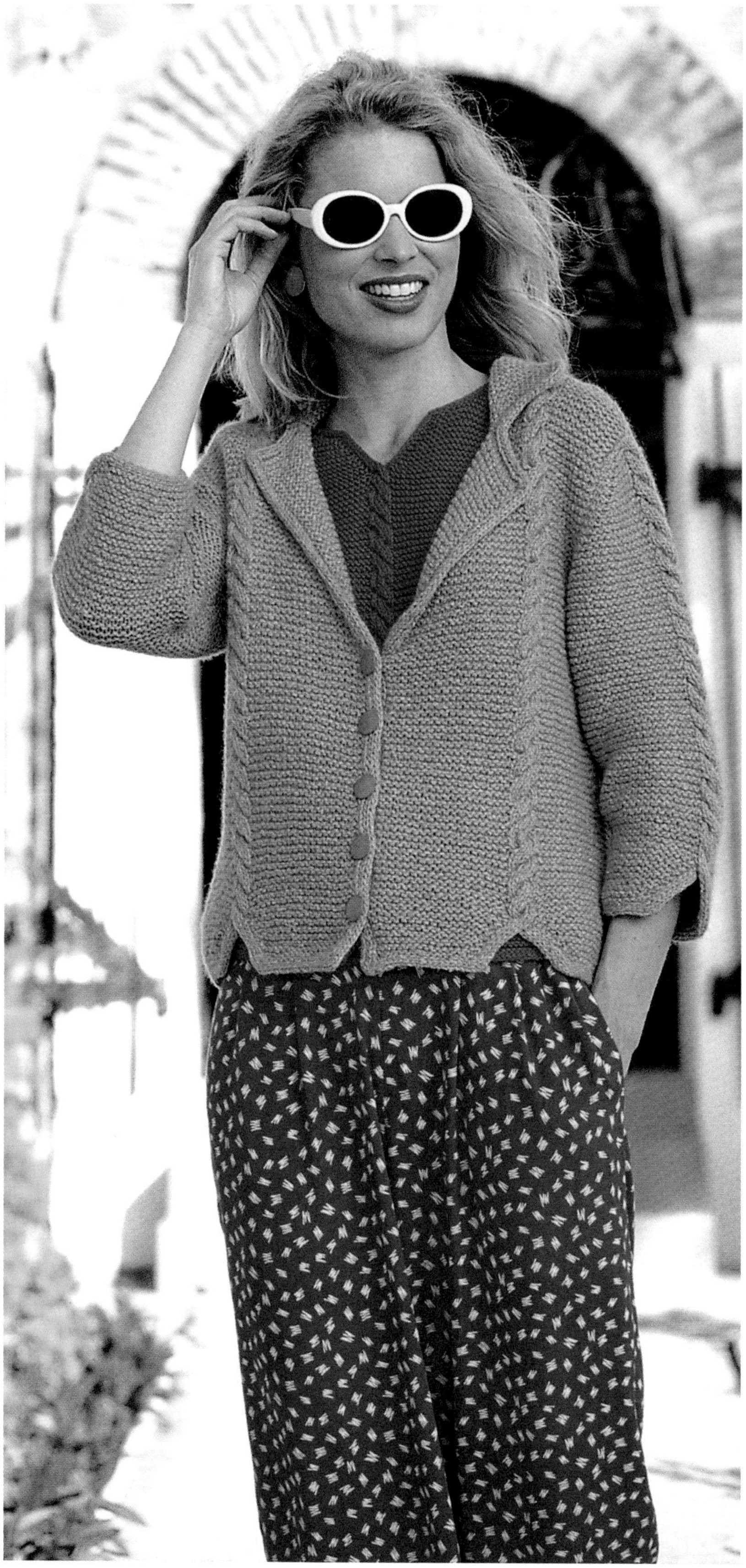

# cropped, curved
## & catty-cornered

Although this might seem like a complicated jacket, with the border traveling around the perimeter of the design, it is surprisingly easy to knit.

# roundtrip

**INTERMEDIATE**

**LOOSE FIT**

**S/M (L/1X)**
**Shown in Small/Medium**
**A** 46 (50)"
**B** 21 (21)"
**C** 24 (24¼)"

Multicolored jacket
Solid blue jacket
**10cm/4"**

**26/18**

**16/11**

• over stockinette stitch (knit on RS, purl on WS), using size 4.5mm/US 7; 6.5mm/US 10½

1 2 3 **4** 5 6

• Medium weight
• 1100 (1100) yds color matching
• 880 (975) yds no color matching

1 2 3 4 **5** 6

• Bulky weight
• 724 (784) yds

• 4.5mm/US 7; 6.5mm/US 10½, 40cm (16") and 60cm (24") long

Two dpn (same size as working needles)

**&**

• Stitch marker and holder

**yarn**
NORO Kureyon (wool; 50g; 110 yds) multicolor brights
NASHUA Wooly Stripes (wool; 50g; 88 yds) multicolor orange
LION BRAND Kool Wool (wool blend; 50g; 60 yds) blue
KNIT ONE CROCHET TOO Paint Box (wool; 50g; 100 yds) multicolor blues

## Notes

**1** See *School*, page 94, for SSK, SSSK, invisible cast-on, and 3-needle bind-off. **2** Use invisible cast-on throughout. **3** For the multicolored jackets, you may choose to purchase extra yarn to make it easier to match colors when joining new balls of yarn.

## MULTICOLORED JACKET

### 1 Center Back

Cast on 64 (74) stitches. *Row 1* (WS) Purl. *Row 2* K1, k2tog, knit to last 3 stitches, SSK, k1. Repeat these 2 rows 15 (19) times more—32 (34) stitches. Work 92 (84) rows even (124 rows total). Piece measures approximately 19" from beginning. Place stitches on hold. Break yarn.

### 2 Garter Band (on rainbow jacket, see above)

With double-pointed needles (dpns), cast on 10 stitches. Knit 239 rows (120 garter ridges). Place 64 (74) cast-on stitches of center back on circular needle.

### 3 *Join band to lower center back*

*Row 1* (RS) With dpn, knit 9 band stitches, then with RS of center back facing, SSK (one stitch of band together with one stitch from center back cast-on), turn. *Row 2* Knit 10. Repeat these 2 rows until all cast-on stitches have been worked, ending with a WS row.

### 4 Knit 240 rows (120 garter ridges).

### 5 *Join band to top of center back*

*Row 1* (RS) K9, SSK (one stitch from band together with one stitch from center back holder), turn. *Row 2* Knit 10. Repeat these 2 rows until all stitches have been worked from holder.

### 6 Place 10 cast-on stitches of garter band on a dpn and join with open stitches, using 3-needle bind off.

### Right Side (Front, Back, and Sleeve)

### 7 With RS facing, beginning at 12th garter ridge from right side of center back (see diagram on page 62), pick up and knit 12 stitches along band edge (1 stitch in each garter ridge) to edge of center back, 84 stitches along center back edge, and 108 stitches along garter band to starting point—204 stitches.

### 8 Place marker (pm), join and work stockinette stitch (St st) in rounds as follows: *Round 1* * K4, k2tog; repeat from * to end—170 stitches. *Rounds 2 and 4* Knit. *Round 3* SSK, knit to last 2 stitches, k2tog. [Repeat rounds 3 and 4] 9 times more—150 stitches. *Next round* * K3, k2tog; repeat from * to end—120 stitches. Continue in St st (changing to 16" needle when necessary), decreasing 1 stitch each side (as for round 3) every other round 10 times, then every 4th round 18 times—64 stitches. Knit 1 round. Break yarn, leaving a 10" tail. Leave stitches on needle.

### Sleeve Cuff

With dpn, cast on 10 stitches. *Row 1* (RS) K9, then with RS of sleeve facing, SSSK (one stitch from cuff together with 2 stitches from sleeve), turn. *Row 2* Knit 10. Repeat these 2 rows until all sleeve stitches have been worked. Join band stitches as before. Close up hole, using 10" tail.

### Left Side

With RS facing, beginning at 12th garter ridge from left side of center back, pick up and knit 108 stitches along garter band to edge of center back, 84 stitches along center back edge, and 12 stitches along garter band to starting point—204 stitches. Work as for right side.

### Finishing

Block piece.

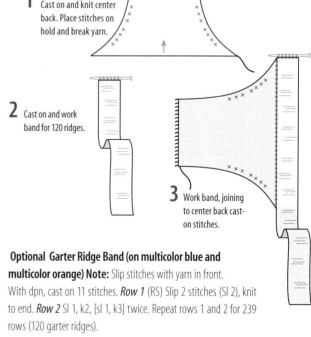

**1** Cast on and knit center back. Place stitches on hold and break yarn.

**2** Cast on and work band for 120 ridges.

**3** Work band, joining to center back cast-on stitches.

### Optional Garter Ridge Band (on multicolor blue and multicolor orange) Note: Slip stitches with yarn in front.

With dpn, cast on 11 stitches. *Row 1* (RS) Slip 2 stitches (Sl 2), knit to end. *Row 2* Sl 1, k2, [sl 1, k3] twice. Repeat rows 1 and 2 for 239 rows (120 garter ridges).

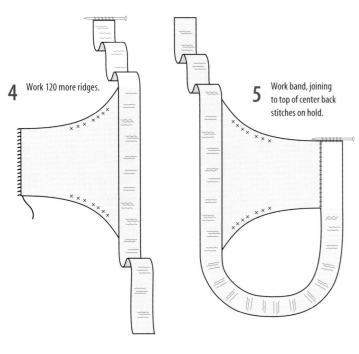

**4** Work 120 more ridges.

**5** Work band, joining to top of center back stitches on hold.

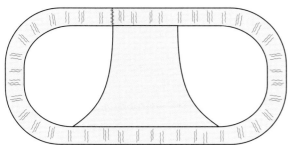

**6** Join band cast-on to stitches on needle.

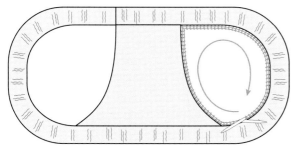

**7** Pick up stitches for right side around inside of band and along back.

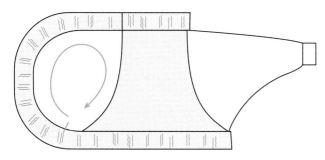

**8** Knit right side and sleeve cuff. Repeat Steps 7 and 8 for left side.

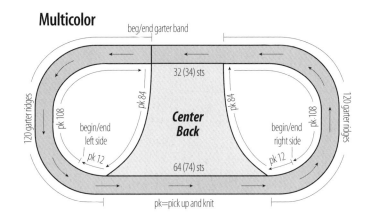

**Multicolor**

beg/end garter band

32 (34) sts

pk 108

pk 84

pk 84

pk 108

120 garter ridges

120 garter ridges

**Center Back**

begin/end left side

begin/end right side

pk 12

pk 12

64 (74) sts

pk=pick up and knit

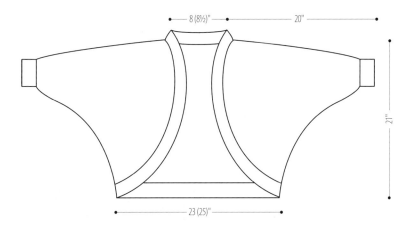

8 (8½)"

20"

21"

23 (25)"

## BLUE JACKET

### Ridge Pattern

*Rounds 1–3* Purl. *Rounds 4–8* Knit. *Round 9* Purl. *Rounds 10–14* Knit. Repeat rounds 1–14 for Ridge Pattern.

### Center Back

Cast on 44 (52) stitches. *Row 1* (WS) Purl. *Row 2* K1, k2tog, knit to last 3 stitches, SSK, k1. Repeat these 2 rows 10 (13) times more—22 (24) stitches. Work 62 (56) rows even (84 rows total). Piece measures approximately 19" from beginning. Place stitches on hold. Break yarn.

### Garter Band

With dpn, cast on 7 stitches. Knit 163 rows (82 garter ridges). Place 44 (52) cast-on stitches of center back on circular needle.

*Join band to lower center back*

*Row 1* (RS) With dpn, knit 6 band stitches, then with RS of center back facing, SSK (one stitch of band together with one stitch from center back cast-on), turn. *Row 2* Knit 7. Repeat these 2 rows until all cast-on stitches have been worked, ending with a WS row. Knit 164 rows (82 garter ridges).

*Join band to top of center back*

*Row 1* (RS) K6, SSK (one stitch of band together with one stitch from center back holder), turn. *Row 2* K7. Repeat these 2 rows until all stitches have been worked from holder. Place 7 cast-on stitches of garter band on a dpn and join with open stitches, using 3-needle bind off.

### Right Side (Front, Back and Sleeve)

With RS facing, beginning at 8th garter ridge from right side of center back (see diagram), pick up and knit 8 stitches along band edge (1 stitch in each garter ridge) to edge of center back, 58 stitches along center back edge, and 74 stitches along garter band to starting point—140 stitches. Place marker (pm), join, and work in rounds as follows: *Next round* * K4, k2tog; repeat from *, end k2—117 stitches. Knit 1 round. *Begin Ridge Pattern and decreases: Round 1* SSK, work round 1 of Ridge Pattern to last 2 stitches, k2tog. *Rounds 2 and 4* K1, work in pattern to last stitch, k1. *Rounds 3 and 5* SSK, work in pattern to last 2 stitches, k2tog. Continue in Ridge Pattern, decreasing 1 stitch at each end of round every other round 3 times more (keep 1 stitch at each end in St st on rounds without decreases)—105 stitches. Work 1 round even. *Next round* * K3, k2tog; repeat from * to end—84 stitches. Continue in Ridge Pattern (changing to 16" needle when necessary), decreasing 1 stitch at each end of round every other round 9 times, then every 4th round 11 times—44 stitches. Knit 3 rounds. Break yarn, leaving a 10" tail. Leave stitches on needle.

### Sleeve Cuff

With dpn, cast on 7 stitches. *Row 1* (RS) K6, then with RS of sleeve facing, SSSK (one stitch from cuff together with 2 stitches from sleeve), turn. *Row 2* Knit 7. Repeat these 2 rows until all sleeve stitches have been worked. Join cuff stitches as before. Close up hole, using 10" tail.

### Left Side

With RS facing, beginning at 8th garter ridge from left side of center back, pick up and knit 74 stitches along garter band to edge of center back, 58 stitches along center back edge, and 8 stitches along garter band to starting point—140 stitches. Work as for right side.

### Finishing

Block piece.

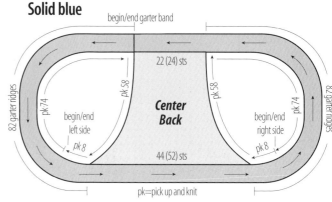

**Solid blue**

begin/end garter band

82 garter ridges

pk 74     pk 58     22 (24) sts     pk 58     pk 74

begin/end left side     **Center Back**     begin/end right side

82 garter ridges

pk 8     44 (52) sts     pk 8

pk=pick up and knit

Lily M. Chin

*This lovely camisole and bolero make a nice set for day or night wear. As the camisole is small and worn next to the skin, a luxury yarn such as this cashmere and silk blend is ideal. If cabling is your favorite brand of knitting, you'll find this pair a pleasure. The matching bolero is a fitting cover-up that turns this from a nighttime beauty into a refined, ladylike look.*

**ADVANCED**

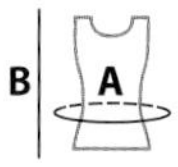

**VERY CLOSE FIT**

**Sizes XS (S, M, L)**
**Shown in Small**

**Camisole**
**A** 32 (34, 36, 38)"
**B** 17 (18, 19, 20)"

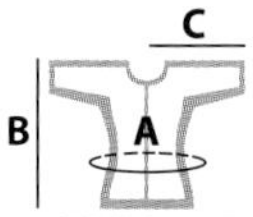

**STANDARD FIT**

**Bolero**
**Cuff to cuff** 53½ (55, 55½, 57)"
**Length to shoulder** 13¾ (14¼, 14¾, 15¼)"

**10cm/4"**
**46/28**
**36/20**

**Camisole • over Chart A, using smaller needles**
**Bolero • over stockinette stitch (knit on RS, purl on WS)**

**1** 2 3 4 5 6

**• Super fine weight**
**Camisole •** 819 (910, 1020, 1130) yds

1 2 **3** 4 5 6

**• Light weight**
**Bolero •** 725 (785, 825, 890) yds

**Camisole •** 2.75mm/US 2 and 3.25mm/US 3, or size to obtain gauge
**Bolero •** 4.5mm/US 7, or size to obtain gauge

**Camisole •** 2.25mm/B-1

**&**
• cable needle (cn)
• stitch markers

# moody blues duo

## CAMISOLE

**Note** See *School*, page 94, for single crochet.

### Front

With larger needles, cast on 149 (158, 167, 176) stitches. *Begin Chart Patterns: Row 1* (RS) K1, work Chart A over 3 (6, 9, 12) stitches, place marker (pm), work 7 stitches Chart B, pm, 5 stitches Chart BB, pm, 7 stitches Chart CC, pm, 9 stitches Chart DD, pm, 11 stitches Chart EE, pm, 9 stitches Chart DD, pm, 7 stitches Chart CC, pm, 5 stitches Chart BB, pm, 7 stitches Chart B, pm, work Chart A over 6 (9, 12, 15) stitches, pm, 7 stitches Chart F, pm, 5 stitches Chart FF, pm, 7 stitches Chart GG, pm, 9 stitches Chart HH, pm, 11 stitches Chart II, pm, 9 stitches Chart HH, pm, 7 stitches Chart GG, pm, 5 stitches Chart FF, pm, 7 stitches Chart F, pm, Chart A over 3 (6, 9, 12) stitches, k1 through back loop (tbl), k1. *Row 2* P1, p1 tbl, work Chart A over 3 (6, 9, 12) stitches, 7 stitches Chart F, 5 stitches Chart FF, 7 stitches Chart GG, 9 stitches Chart HH, 11 stitches Chart II, 9 stitches Chart HH, 7 stitches Chart GG, 5 stitches Chart FF, 7 stitches Chart F, Chart A over 6 (9, 12, 15) stitches, 7 stitches Chart B, 5 stitches Chart BB, 7 stitches Chart CC, 9 stitches Chart DD, 11 stitches Chart EE, 9 stitches Chart DD, 7 stitches Chart CC, 5 stitches Chart BB, 7 stitches Chart B, Chart A over 3 (6, 9, 12) stitches, p1. Continue in chart patterns as established until piece measures 1 (1½, 2, 2)" from beginning. Change to smaller needles. Work until piece measures 4 (4½, 5, 5)" from beginning, end with a WS row.

*Begin bust shaping*

*Increase Row 1* (RS) * Work to Chart BB, work chart over 5 stitches, purling into front and back (pf&b) of each purl stitch (converting it to Chart B); repeat from * once more, ** work to Chart FF, work chart over 5 stitches, pf&b of each purl stitch (converting it to Chart F); repeat from ** once more, work to end—157 (166, 175, 184) stitches. Work 11 rows in newly established patterns. *Increase Row 2* (RS) * Work to Chart CC, work chart over 7 stitches, pf&b of each purl stitch (converting it to Chart C); repeat from * once more, ** work to Chart GG, work chart over 7 stitches, pf&b of each purl stitch (converting it to Chart G); repeat from ** once more, work to end—165 (174, 183, 192) stitches. Work 11 rows in newly established patterns. *Increase Row 3* (RS) * Work to Chart DD, work chart over 9 stitches, pf&b of each purl stitch (converting it to Chart D); repeat from * once more, ** work to Chart HH, work chart over 9 stitches, pf&b of each purl stitch (converting it to Chart H); repeat from ** once more, work to end—173 (182, 191, 200) stitches. Work 11 rows in newly established patterns. *Increase Row 4* (RS) Work to Chart EE, work chart over 11 stitches, pf&b of each purl stitch (converting it to Chart E), work to Chart II, work chart over 11 stitches, pf&b of each

purl stitch (converting it to Chart I), work to end—177 (186, 195, 204) stitches. Work in newly established patterns until piece measures 10½ (11, 11½, 12)" from beginning, end with a WS row.

*Shape armholes and neck*

Bind off 12 (12, 13, 13) stitches at beginning of next 2 rows, 7 (8, 9, 9) stitches at beginning of next 2 rows, 5 (6, 6, 7) stitches at beginning of next 2 rows, 4 (4, 4, 5) stitches at beginning of next 2 rows, 2 stitches at beginning of next 2 rows. Decrease 1 stitch each side on next row, then every other row 6 (7, 8, 9) times more, AT SAME TIME, when armhole measures 2", end with a WS row and work as follows: Mark center 33 (36, 39, 42) stitches. *Begin neck shaping: Next row* (RS) Continue to decrease at armhole edge, work to center marked stitches, join 2nd ball of yarn and bind off stitches between markers, work to end. Continue in patterns, binding off at each neck edge 6 stitches once, 4 stitches once, 2 stitches once. Decrease 1 stitch at each neck edge every RS row 7 times—16 stitches each side. Work even until armhole measures 6½ (7, 7½, 8)". Bind off.

### Back

Work as for front until piece measures same length as front to underarm.

*Shape armholes and neck*

*Next row* (RS) Bind off 12 (12, 13, 13) stitches, work until there are 60 (63, 65, 68) stitches on right needle, join 2nd ball of yarn and bind off center 33 (36, 39, 42) stitches, work to end. Continue to shape armholes and neck as for front—16 stitches each side. Work even until armhole measures same length as front to shoulder. Bind off.

### Finishing

Block pieces. Sew shoulders. Sew side seams. Work single crochet around armhole and neck edges.

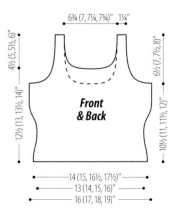

*Front & Back*

6¾ (7, 7¼, 7¾)" 1¼"
4½ (5, 5½, 6)"
6½ (7, 7½, 8)"
12½ (13, 13½, 14)"
10½ (11, 11½, 12)"
14 (15, 16½, 17½)"
13 (14, 15, 16)"
16 (17, 18, 19)"

**BOLERO** K1 C2 Creme Brulee DK (wool; 50g; 131 yds) blue
**CAMISOLE** Richesse et Soie (cashmere, silk; 25g; 145 yds) blue
*original yarn*

**Chart A**

2
1
3-st rep

**Chart B**

2
1
7 sts

**Chart BB**

2
1
5 sts

**Chart C**
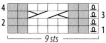
4
2
3
1
9 sts

**Chart CC**

4
2
3
1
7 sts

**Chart D**
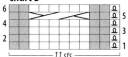
6
4
2
5
3
1
11 sts

**Chart DD**
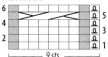
6
4
2
5
3
1
9 sts

**Chart E**
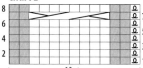
8
6
4
2
7
5
3
1
13 sts

**Chart EE**
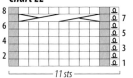
8
6
4
2
7
5
3
1
11 sts

**Chart F**

2
1
7 sts

**Chart FF**

2
1
5 sts

**Chart G**
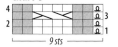
4
2
3
1
9 sts

**Chart GG**

4
2
3
1
7 sts

**Chart H**
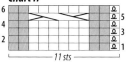
6
4
2
5
3
1
11 sts

**Chart HH**
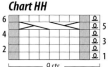
6
4
2
5
3
1
9 sts

**Chart I**
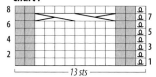
8
6
4
2
7
5
3
1
13 sts

**Chart II**
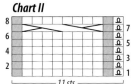
8
6
4
2
7
5
3
1
11 sts

**Chart J**

4
2
3
1
6 sts

**Chart K**

4
2
3
1
6 sts

**Stitch key**
- ☐ Knit on RS, purl on WS
- ▨ Purl on RS, knit on WS
- Ω K1 tbl on RS, p1 tbl on WS
- ⤬ 1/1 RC  Sl 1 to cn, hold to back, k1; k1 from cn.
- ⤬ 1/1 LC  Sl 1 to cn, hold to front, k1; k1 from cn.
- ⤬ 2/2 RC  Sl 2 to cn, hold to back, k2; k2 from cn.
- ⤬ 2/2 LC  Sl 2 to cn, hold to front, k2; k2 from cn.
- ⤬ 3/3 RC  Sl 3 to cn, hold to back, k3; k3 from cn.
- ⤬ 3/3 LC  Sl 3 to cn, hold to front, k3; k3 from cn.
- ⤬ 4/4 RC  Sl 4 to cn, hold to back, k4; k4 from cn.
- ⤬ 4/4 LC  Sl 4 to cn, hold to front, k4; k4 from cn.

**Camisole Arrangement**

| | | | inc 1 | inc 2 | inc 3 | inc 4 | inc 3 | inc 2 | inc 1 | | | | inc 1 | inc 2 | inc 3 | inc 4 | inc 3 | inc 2 | inc 1 | |
|---|---|---|---|---|---|---|---|---|---|---|---|---|---|---|---|---|---|---|---|---|
| | | | 7 sts F | 9 sts G | 11 sts H | 13 sts I | 11 sts H | 9 sts G | 7 sts F | | | | 7 sts B | 9 sts C | 11 sts D | 13 sts E | 11 sts D | 9 sts C | 7 sts B | * = stitch marker |
| 1 St st selvage | K1 tbl, (RS) P1 tbl, (WS) | 3(6,9,12) sts A | 7 sts F | 5 sts FF | 7 sts GG | 9 sts HH | 11 sts II | 9 sts HH | 7 sts GG | 5 sts FF | 7 sts F | 6(9,12,15) sts A | 7 sts B | 5 sts BB | 7 sts CC | 9 sts DD | 11 sts EE | 9 sts DD | 7 sts CC | 5 sts BB | 7 sts B | 3(6,9,12) sts A | 1 St st selvage |
| | | * | * | * | * | * | * | * | * | * | * | * | * | * | * | * | * | * | * | * | * |

## BOLERO

**Notes 1** See *School*, page 94 for wrapping stitches on short rows and cable cast-on. **2** Bolero is worked in one piece from right cuff to left cuff.

### Right Sleeve

Cast on 44 (48, 52, 56) stitches. *Begin K2, P2 Rib and Chart J: Row 1* (RS) P0 (2, 0, 2), [k2, p2] 4 (4, 5, 5) times, k2, p1, place marker (pm), work 6 stitches Chart J, pm, p1, [k2, p2] 4 (5, 5, 6) times, k2 (0, 2, 0). Continue in rib and cable patterns as established until rib measures 1", end with a WS row. *Next row* (RS) Knit to marker, work 6 stitches Chart J between markers, knit to end. Continue working Chart J between markers and stockinette stitch at each side, AT SAME TIME, increase 1 stitch each side every 4th row 12 times, then every 6th row 8 times—84 (88, 92, 96). Work even until piece measures 15½" from beginning, end with a WS row.

*Body and right sleeve cap*

(**Note:** Slip stitches purlwise with yarn in front.)

*Next row* (RS) Cable cast on 25 stitches (right front), then knit to marked stitches, work 6 stitches Chart J, knit to end. *Next row* (WS) Cable cast on 33 stitches (right back), then sl 1, p2, pm, work Chart J over 6 stitches, pm, work in pattern to end—142 (146, 150, 154). * *Next row* Work in pattern to last 3 stitches, k3. *Next row* Sl 1, p2, work in pattern to end. Repeat from * twice more. *Begin short-row shaping: Row 1* (RS) Bind off 3 (4, 4, 5) stitches, work to last 38 stitches, wrap next stitch and turn (W&T). *Row 2* (WS) Work to last 27 (26, 26, 25) stitches, W&T. *Row 3* Work 71 (74, 78, 82) stitches, W&T. *Row 4* Work 68 (70, 74, 78) stitches, W&T. *Row 5* Work 65 (67, 70, 74) stitches, W&T. *Row 6* Work 62 (64, 66, 70) stitches, W&T. *Row 7* Work 58 (60, 63, 66) stitches, W&T. *Row 8* Work 54 (56, 60, 62) stitches, W&T. *Row 9* Work 51 (53, 56, 58) stitches, W&T. *Row 10* Work 48 (50, 52, 54) stitches, W&T. *Row 11* Work 45 (46, 48, 50) stitches, W&T. *Row 12* Work 42 (42, 44, 46) stitches, W&T. *Row 13* Work 38 (39, 41, 42) stitches, W&T. *Row 14* Work 34 (36, 38, 38) stitches, W&T. *Row 15* Work 31 (32, 34, 34) stitches, W&T. *16* Work 28 (28, 30, 30) stitches, W&T. *Row 17* Work 25 (25, 26, 26) stitches, W&T. *Row 18* Work 22 stitches, W&T. *Row 19* Work 18 stitches, W&T. *Row 20* Work 14 stitches, W&T. *Next 2 rows* Work to end of row, hiding wraps—139 (142, 146, 149) stitches.

*Shape right front edge*

Bind off at front edge (beginning of RS rows) as follows: *Size XS* 4 stitches twice, [4 stitches twice, 3 stitches once] 4 times, 4 stitches once—83 stitches; *Size S* [3 stitches once, 4 stitches once] 6 times, 3 stitches 5 times—85 stitches; *Size M* 4 stitches once, 3 stitches once, 4 stitches 4 times, [3 stitches once, 4 stitches once] 3 times, 3 stitches 5 times—87 stitches; *Size L* [3 stitches twice, 4 stitches once] twice, 3 stitches 13 times—90 stitches.

*All Sizes* End with a WS row.

*Shape back neck*

*Decrease Row* (RS) Bind off 3 (3, 3, 4) stitches, work to 2nd marker, k2tog, work to end. Continue to decrease 1 stitch after 2nd marker every other row 4 times more—75 (77, 79, 81) stitches. Work 9 (11, 13, 14) rows even. From this point, substitute Chart K for Chart J. Work 1 row and mark it for center back neck. Work 9 (11, 13, 14) rows even. *Increase Row* (RS) Work to 2nd marker, knit into front and back of next stitch, work to end. Repeat Increase Row every other row 4 times more—80 (82, 84, 86) stitches. Work 1 row even.

*Shape left front edge*

*Next row* (RS) Cable cast on 3 (3, 3, 4) stitches, work to end—83 (85, 87, 90) stitches. Continue in pattern, cast on at front edge (beginning of RS rows): *Size XS* 4 stitches once, [3 stitches once, 4 stitches twice] 4 times, 4 stitches twice—139 stitches; *Size S* 3 stitches 5 times, [4 stitches once, 3 stitches once] 6 times—142 stitches; *Size M* 3 stitches 5 times, [4 stitches once, 3 stitches once] 3 times, 4 stitches 4 times, 3 stitches once, 4 stitches once—146 stitches; *Size L* 3 stitches 13 times, [4 stitches once, 3 stitches twice] twice—149 stitches.

*Left sleeve cap*

*Begin short rows: Row 1* (WS) Work 82 (84, 86, 88) stitches, W&T. *Row 2* (RS) Work 14 stitches, W&T. (**Note** For remaining rows, hide wraps of previous rows as you come to them.) *Row 3* Work 18 stitches, W&T. *Row 4* Work 22 stitches, W&T. *Row 5* Work 25 (25, 26, 26) stitches, W&T. *Row 6* Work 28 (28, 30, 30) stitches, W&T. *Row 7* Work 31 (32, 34, 34) stitches, W&T. *Row 8* Work 34 (36, 38, 38) stitches, W&T. *Row 9* Work 38 (39, 41, 42) stitches, W&T. *Row 10* Work 42 (42, 44, 46) stitches, W&T. *Row 11* Work 45 (46, 48, 50) stitches, W&T. *Row 12* Work 48 (50, 52, 54) stitches, W&T. *Row 13* Work 51 (53, 56, 58) stitches, W&T. *Row 14* Work 54 (56, 60, 62) stitches, W&T. *Row 15* Work 58 (60, 63, 66) stitches, W&T. *Row 16* Work 62 (64, 66, 70) stitches, W&T. *Row 17* Work 65 (67, 70, 74) stitches, W&T. *Row 18* Work 68 (70, 74, 78) stitches, W&T. *Row 19* Work 71 (74, 78, 82) stitches, W&T. *Row 20* Work 74 (78, 82, 86) stitches, W&T. *Next row* (WS) Work to end of row. *Next row* (RS) Cast on 3 (4, 4, 5) stitches, work to end, hiding remaining wrap—142 (146, 150, 154) stitches. Work even for 1", end with a RS row. *Next row* (WS) Bind off 33 stitches, work to end. *Next row* Bind off 25 stitches, work to end—84 (88, 92, 96) stitches.

### Left Sleeve

Work even for ¾", end with a WS row. Continue in pattern, decreasing 1 stitch each side on next row, then every 6th row 8 times, then every 4th row 11 times—44 (48, 52, 56) stitches. Work 5 rows even. *Begin Rib Pattern and Chart K:* Row 1 (RS) P0 (2, 0, 2), [k2, p2] 4 (4, 5, 5) times, k2, p1, work 6 stitches Chart K, p1, [k2, p2] 4 (5, 5, 6) times, k2 (0, 2, 0). Continue in rib and cable patterns as established until rib measures 1", end with a WS row. Bind off in pattern.

### Finishing

Block pieces. Sew side and sleeve seams, leaving last 10 stitches of back and 1 front stitch unsewn.

*Front trim*

With RS facing, pick up and knit the last 10 stitches of back at right side edge. *Next row* (WS) P1, pm, work 6 stitches of Chart J, pm, p2, sl 1. *Next row* K3, work in pattern to last stitch, k1. *Next row* P1, work in pattern between markers, p2, sl 1. Repeat last 2 rows until trim is long enough to reach center back neck marker. Substitute Chart K for Chart J, beginning on same pattern row. Work until trim is long enough to reach left side edge. Bind off. Sew trim along front edge. Sew bound-off edge of trim to bound-off edge of left side cable.

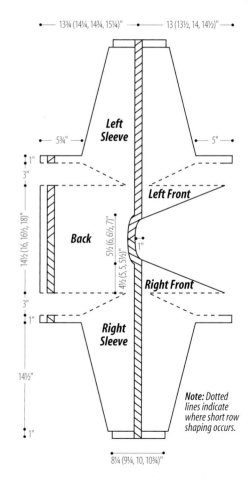

← 13¾ (14¼, 14¾, 15¼)" → ← 13 (13½, 14, 14½)" →

← 5¾" →   ← 5" →

Left Sleeve

Left Front

Back

Right Front

Right Sleeve

1"

3"

14½ (16, 16½, 18)"

5½ (6, 6½, 7)"

4½ (5, 5, 5½)"

1"

3"

1"

14½"

1"

8¼ (9¼, 10, 10¾)"

*Note: Dotted lines indicate where short row shaping occurs.*

*Elegant, day or night, says it all about this special twinset. The unusually shaped jacket and sleek under-tank are great whether worn alone or combined. The combination of wool and silk yarns in solid and tweed adds extra interest.*

Debra M. Lee

# glamour in ribbing

**EXPERIENCED**

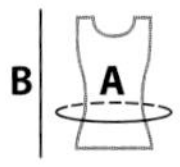

**VERY CLOSE FIT**

**Sizes S (M, L, 1X)**
**Tank**
**Shown in Medium**
A 34 (36, 38½, 40)"
B 23½ (24, 25½, 26)"

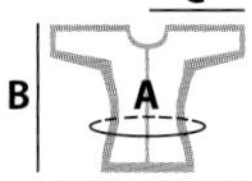

**STANDARD FIT**

**Jacket**
**Shown in Medium**
Center Back length 18 (18, 18¼, 18¼)"
Cuff to cuff 64 (64¾, 67½, 68½)"

**10cm/4"**
**25/22**
**21/20**
Tank • over stockinette stitch (knit every round)
Jacket • over K2, P2 rib

1 2 3 4 5 6

• **Medium weight**
Tank MC • 625 (675, 765, 815) yds
CC • 110 (110, 110, 110) yds
Jacket • 1275 (1320, 1385, 1415) yds

Tank • 4.5mm/US 7, or size to obtain gauge, 60cm/24" long
Jacket • 5mm/US 8, or size to obtain gauge, 91cm/36" and 112cm/44" long

Tank • two 4mm/US 6

Tank • 5mm/H-8

**&**
Tank • stitch holders
Both • stitch markers

## TANK

### Notes

**1** See *School*, page 94 for SSK, 3-needle bind-off, and grafting open stitches to cast-on edge. **2** Tank is knit circularly to armhole, then divided for front and back, which are worked in rows.

### Body

With crochet hook and CC, chain 254 (270, 286, 294) stitches. Then with circular needle and MC, pick up and knit 254 (270, 286, 294) stitches in back loops of chain (as shown on page 69).

Place marker and join, being careful not to twist stitches. **Begin Rib Pattern: Round 1** * K1 through back loop (tbl), p1; repeat from * around, placing a 2nd marker after 127th (135th, 143rd, 147th) stitch for side "seam." Continue in Rib Pattern until piece measures 8 (8, 8½, 8¾)" from beginning. **Next round** Knit to marker, decreasing 38 (40, 42, 42) stitches evenly across—89 (95, 101, 105) stitches (for back), work in Rib Pattern to end—127 (135, 143, 147) stitches (for front). Continue working 89 (95, 101, 105) stitches for back in stockinette stitch, AT SAME TIME, work stitches for front as follows: (**Note:** Pattern is a repeat of 8 rounds, with 7 additional knit stitches worked before and after Rib Pattern on every 8-round repeat.) **Round 1** K1, SSK, rib to last 3 stitches, k2tog, k1. **Round 2** K2, rib to last 2 stitches, k2. **Round 3** K2, SSK, rib to last 4 stitches, k2tog, k2. **Round 4** K4, rib to last 4 stitches, k4. **Round 5** K5, SSK, rib to last 7 stitches, k2tog, k5. **Round 6** K6, rib to last 6 stitches, k6. **Round 7** K7, rib to last 7 stitches, k7. **Round 8** K8, rib to last 8 stitches, k8. **Round 9** K8, SSK, rib to last 10 stitches, k2tog, k8. **Round 10** K9, rib to last 9 stitches, k9. **Round 11** K9, SSK, rib to last 11 stitches, k2tog, k9. **Round 12** K11, rib to last 11 stitches, k11. **Round 13** K12, SSK, rib to last 14 stitches, k2tog, k12. **Round 14** K13, rib to last 13 stitches, k13. **Round 15** K14, rib to last 14 stitches, k14. **Round 16** K15, rib to last 15 stitches, k15. Continue to repeat rounds 1-8, adding 7 knit stitches before and after Rib Pattern on each 8-round repeat 4 (4, 4, 5) times more, then work first 1 (4, 7, 0) rounds once more—89 (95, 101, 105) stitches. **Size 1X: Next round** K51, p1, k1 tbl, p1, k51. **All Sizes: Next round** Knit. Piece measures approximately 16 (16½, 17½, 18)" from beginning.

*Divide for front and back*

**Next row** (RS) Bind off 5 (5, 5, 6) stitches, knit to end of back, place front stitches on hold, turn. **Next row** Bind off 5 (5, 5, 6) stitches, purl to end of back.

## Back

*Shape armholes*

Decrease 1 stitch each side every RS row 1 (9, 17, 17) times, then alternately [on 4th row, then on 2nd row] 6 (4, 1, 1) times, then on 4th row 1 (0, 1, 1) time—51 (51, 51, 53) stitches. Work 1 row even. Armhole measures approximately 7 (7, 7½, 7½)".

*Shape neck*

**Next row** (RS) K11, join 2nd ball of yarn and bind off next 29 (29, 29, 31) stitches, knit to end. Working both sides at same time, decrease 1 stitch at each neck edge on next RS row. Work 1 row even. Place remaining 10 stitches each side on hold.

## Front

Join yarn at underarm and shape armholes as for back until 59 (59, 59, 61) stitches remain, end with a WS row. Mark center 11 (11, 11, 13) stitches.

*Shape neck*

Continue to shape armholes as for back, AT SAME TIME, with 2nd ball of yarn, bind off marked stitches and, working both sides at same time, bind off from each neck edge 3 stitches once, 2 stitches once. Decrease 1 stitch each side every RS row 5 times—10 stitches each side. Work 1 row even. Place stitches on hold.

## Finishing

Join shoulders using 3-needle bind-off.

*Neck edging*

With RS facing, dpn, and CC, work 3-stitch attached I-cord around neck edge. Graft open stitches to cast-on edge.

*Armhole edging*

Work as for neck edging.

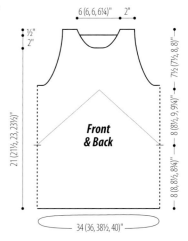

6 (6, 6, 6¼)"    2"
½"
2"
21 (21½, 23, 23½)"
7½ (7½, 8, 8)"
8 (8½, 9, 9¼)"
8 (8, 8½, 8¾)"

**Front & Back**

34 (36, 38½, 40)"

**JACKET** MUENCH/HORSTIA Tweed (wool; 50g; 110 yds) Gray-blue
**TANK** MUENCH/HORSTIA Maulbeerseide/Schurwolle (silk; wool; 50g; 110 yds) Cadet Blue (MC)
*original yarn* Tweed (wool; 50g; 110 yds) Gray-blue (CC)

## JACKET

### Notes

**1** See *School*, page 94, for wrapping stitches on short rows. **2** Jacket is worked in one piece from top of collar to lower back.

### Collar

With 36" needle, cast on 260 (268, 276, 284) stitches loosely. *Begin Rib Pattern: Row 1* * K2, p2; repeat from * to end. Repeat row 1 until collar measures 5", end with a WS row. *Decrease row* (RS) * K2tog; repeat from * to end—130 (134, 138, 142) stitches.

### Body

*Next row* (WS) * P2, k2; repeat from *, end p2. *Begin short-row shaping: Row 1* Rib 9 (5, 9, 9), wrap next stitch and turn (W&T). *Row 2 and all even-numbered rows* Work even in pattern. *Row 3* Rib 17 (13, 17, 17), hiding wrap when you come to it, W&T. *Row 5* Rib 21 (21, 25, 25), W&T. *Row 7* Rib 25 (29, 33, 33), W&T. *Row 9* Rib 37 (41, 45, 45), W&T. *Row 11* Rib 49 (53, 57, 57), W&T. *Row 13* Rib 61 (65, 67, 69), W&T. *Row 15* Work across all stitches. Repeat rows 1–15 once more for other side.

*Shape sleeves*

Change to 44" needle and place a marker (pm) at each end of needle (for ease in counting later). Continue in pattern, casting on 7 stitches (working added stitches into pattern) at end of next 6 (6, 18, 18) rows, 6 stitches at end of next 18 (18, 4, 4) rows, 5 stitches at end of next 0 (0, 2, 2) rows, 20 stitches at end of next 2 rows—95 (95, 100, 100) stitches from marker each side for sleeve. Work even for 46 (46, 50, 50) rows. Bind off 20 stitches at beginning of next 2 rows, 5 stitches at beginning of next 0 (0, 2, 2) rows, 6 stitches at beginning of next 18 (18, 4, 4) rows, 7 stitches at beginning of next 6 (6, 18, 18) rows—130 (134, 138, 142) stitches. Remove markers.

*Lower Back*

Work even for 42 rows. *Begin short-row shaping: Row 1* (RS) Rib 125 (129, 133, 137), W&T. *Row 2* Rib 120 (124, 128, 132), W&T. *Row 3* Rib 104 (108, 112, 116), W&T. *Row 4* Rib 88 (92, 96, 100), W&T. *Row 5* Rib 64 (68, 72, 76), W&T. *Row 6* Rib 40 (44, 48, 52), W&T. *Rows 7 and 8* Work to end of row, hiding wraps as you come to them. Bind off in pattern.

### Finishing

Block lightly. Sew side and sleeve seams, matching edges of collar to lower back side seams.

### Schematic

Lower Back — 1"

8"

Right Sleeve — Fold line — Left Sleeve

18 (18, 18½, 18½)"

8½ (8½, 9¼, 9¼)"

3"

Collar

5"

19 (19, 20, 20)" — 26 (26¾, 27½, 28½)"

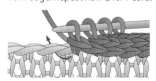

## HOW TO:

### ATTACHED I-CORD EDGING

*Row 1* With dpn, cast on 3 stitches, then pick up and knit 1 stitch along edge of piece—4 stitches.
*Row 2* Slide stitches to opposite end of dpn and k2, then k2tog through the back loops, pick up and knit 1 stitch from edge. Repeat Row 2 for I-cord.

### CHAIN CAST-ON

*If you invest the time to make a cabled jacket, you want to be sure that it's ageless and classic. The beautiful cabled wool creates a rich fabric that is special enough to wear for any occasion.*

*Shirley Paden*

# timeless burgundy

**ADVANCED**

C
B A
**STANDARD FIT**

**Sizes S (M, L)**
**Shown in Small**
**A** 40½ (44¼, 48¼)"
**B** 18 (18½, 19)"
**C** 30 (31, 32)"

**10cm/4"**
35
34
**• over Chart B,**
**using larger needles**

1 2 3  5 6

**• Medium weight**
2445 (2710, 2980) yds

**• 3.5mm/US 4 and 4mm/US 6,**
**or size to obtain gauge**

**• three 20mm/¾"**

**&**
**• cable needle (cn)**
**• stitch holders**
**• stitch markers**

**original yarn**
FILATURA DI CROSA/
STACY CHARLES
COLLECTION Zara (wool;
50g; 136 yds) burgundy

## Notes

**1** See *School*, page 94, for Make (M1) and wrapping stitches on short rows. **2** Work first and last stitch of every row in stockinette stitch (knit on RS, purl on WS), unless otherwise specified.

## 8-row increase in Chart A

*Row 1* (RS) K1, M1, work in pattern to last stitch, M1, k1—2 stitches increased. *Row 2* P1, KPK, work to last 2 stitches, KPK, p1—4 stitches increased. *Rows 3 and 5* Work in pattern as established. *Row 4* P1, p2tog, [k1, p1] in next stitch, work in pattern to last 4 stitches, p2tog, [k1, p1] in next stitch, p1. *Row 6* P1, KPK, p2tog, work in pattern to last 4 stitches, KPK, p2tog, p1—2 stitches increased. *Rows 7 and 8* Work in pattern as established, working 4 new stitches each side in Chart A.

## Back

With larger needles, cast on 158 (174, 190) stitches. *Begin Charts A and B: Row 1* (RS) K1, work 12 (16, 20) stitches Chart A, 54 stitches Chart B, 24 (32, 40) stitches Chart A, 54 stitches Chart B, 12 (16, 20) stitches Chart A, k1. Continue in patterns as established through row 24 of Chart B.

*Shape sides*

Work 8-row increase in Chart A once—166 (182, 198) stitches. Work 12 rows even. Work 8-row increase in Chart A once—174 (190, 206) stitches. Work even until 24 rows of Chart B have been worked 3 times, then work rows 1-6 once more. Piece measures approximately 9".

*Shape armholes*

Bind off 4 stitches at beginning of next 4 (6, 6) rows, 3 stitches at beginning of next 6 rows, 2 stitches at beginning of next 2 (2, 4) rows, 1 stitch at beginning of next 2 rows—134 (142, 154) stitches. Work even until armhole measures 9 (9½, 10)", end with a WS row. Place stitches on hold.

## Right Front

With larger needles, cast on 53 (61, 69) stitches. *Begin Charts A and B: Row 1* (RS) Work stitches 15-54 (11-54, 7-54) of Chart B, then work Chart A over 12 (16, 20) stitches, k1. Continue in chart patterns as established, AT SAME TIME, shape center front edge as follows:

*Shape center front*

**Note:** Work increases at center front into Chart B, then into Chart A.
Cast on 3 stitches at end of every WS row 3 times, then cast on 2 stitches at end of every WS row 3 (3, 1) times—68 (76, 80) stitches. *Size L only* Work 1 row even. *Row 10* (WS) Work in pattern to last 5 stitches, p3tog, KPK, p1, cast on 2 stitches. Work 1 row even. *Row 12* (WS) Work in pattern to last 7 stitches, KPK, p3tog, p3, cast on 2 stitches—84 stitches. *All Sizes: Row 13* (RS) K1, p0 (4, 8), place marker (pm), work in pattern to end. *Row 14* Work in pattern to marker, [p3tog, KPK] 0 (1, 2) times, p1, cast on 1 stitch. *Row 15* K1, p1 (5, 9), work in pat-

tern to end. *Row 16* Work in pattern to marker, [KPK, p3tog] 0 (1, 2) times, KPK, p1. *Rows 17, 19, 21 and 23* Knit into front and back of stitch (kf&b), purl to marker, work in pattern to end. *Row 18* Work in pattern to marker, [p3tog, KPK] 1 (2, 3) times, p1. *Row 20* Work in pattern to marker, [KPK, p3tog] 1 (2, 3) times, KPK, p1. *Row 22* Work in pattern to marker, [p3tog, KPK] 2 (3, 4) times, p1. *Row 24* Work in pattern to marker, [KPK, p3tog] 2 (3, 4) times, KPK, p1. *Next row* Kf&b, purl to marker, work in pattern to last stitch, M1, k1 (row 1 of 8-row increase at side edge). *Next row* P1, KPK, work in pattern to marker, remove marker, work row 4 of Chart A over 12 (16, 20) stitches, p1. Continue in patterns as established (shaping side edge as for back), until 24 rows of Chart B have been worked 3 times, then work rows 1-7 once more—88 (96, 104) stitches.

*Shape armhole and collar*

Shape armhole at side edge as for back, AT SAME TIME, after 79 (83, 87) rows of Chart B have been worked and piece measures approximately 9 (9½, 10)" from beginning, work as follows: *Begin Right Front Collar Chart: Rows 1 and 3* (WS of front and RS of collar) Work in pattern as established for front to last 5 stitches of row, work collar chart over 5 stitches. *Rows 2 and 4* Work collar chart over 5 stitches, work in pattern as established for front to end. Repeat last 4 rows once more. Repeat last 8 rows once, working collar chart over last 9 stitches of WS rows (of front) and first 9 stitches of RS rows (of front). Continue in pattern as established, adding one chart repeat every 8 rows, until there are 37 collar pattern stitches. Work even until armhole measures same length as back to shoulder. *Next row* Work 37 collar stitches and place remaining 31 (35, 41) stitches on hold. *Next row* Cast on 1 stitch for selvage, work to end—38 stitches. Work even until collar measures 4" above shoulder, end with chart row 4.

*Shape top of collar*

*Begin short-row shaping: Row 1* (RS) K9, p28, k1. *Row 2* P1, [p3tog, KPK] 7 times, wrap next stitch and turn (W&T). *Row 3* K8, p20, k1. *Row 4* P1, [KPK, p3tog] 5 times, W&T. *Row 5* K8, p12, k1. *Row 6* P1, [p3tog, KPK] 3 times, W&T. *Row 7* Knit 13. Bind off all stitches purlwise.

## Left Front

With larger needles, cast on 53 (61, 69) stitches. *Begin Charts A and B: Row 1* (RS) K1, work Chart A over 12 (16, 20) stitches, then work stitches 1-40 (1-44, 1-48) of Chart B, then cast on 3 stitches. Continue in chart patterns as established, AT SAME TIME, continue to shape center front edge by casting on 3 stitches at end of every RS row 2 times more, then cast on 2 stitches at end of every RS row 3 (3, 1) times—68 (76, 82) stitches. *Size L only: Row 10* (WS) P3, KPK, p3tog, work to end. *Row 11* Work in pattern to end, cast on 2 stitches—84 stitches. *All Sizes: Row 12* (WS) P1, [p3tog, KPK] 0 (1, 2) times, pm, work to end. *Row 13* (RS) Work to last 1 (5, 9) stitches, p0 (4, 8), k1. *Row 14* P1, [KPK, p3tog] 0 (1, 2) times, work to end. *Row 15: Size S only* Work to marker, M1, k1. *Sizes M, L only* Work to marker, p3 (7), purl into front and back of next stitch (pf&b), k1. *Row 16* P1, KPK, [p3tog, KPK] 0 (1, 2) times, work to end. *Rows 17, 19, 21 and 23* Work to marker, then purl to last 2 stitches, pf&b, k1. *Row 18* P1, [KPK, p3tog] 1 (2, 3) times, work to end. *Row 20* P1, KPK, [p3tog, KPK] 1 (2, 3) times, work to end. *Row 22* P1, [KPK, p3tog] 2 (3, 4) times, work to end. *Row 24* P1, KPK, [p3tog, KPK] 2 (3, 4) times, work to end. *Next row* (RS) K1, M1 (row 1 of 8-row increase at side edge), work to marker, then purl to last 2 stitches, pf&b, k1. *Next row* P1, work row 2 of Chart A over 12 (16, 20) stitches, remove marker, work to last 2 stitches, KPK, p1 (row 2 of 8-row increase). Continue in patterns as established (shaping side edge as for back), until piece measures same length as back to underarm—88 (96, 104) stitches.

*Shape armhole and collar*

Shape armhole at side edge as for back, AT SAME TIME, after 79 (83, 87) rows of Chart B have been worked and piece measures approximately 9 (9½, 10)" from beginning, work as follows: *Begin Left Front Collar Chart: Rows 1 and 3* (WS of front and RS of collar) Work left front collar chart over 5 stitches, then work in pattern as established for front to end. *Rows 2 and 4* Work to last 5 stitches, work collar chart over 5 stitches. Repeat last 4 rows once more. Repeat last 8 rows once, working collar chart over last 9 stitches of RS rows (of front) and first 9 stitches of WS rows (of front). Continue in pattern as established, adding one chart repeat every 8 rows, until there are 37 collar pattern stitches. Work even until armhole measures same length as back to shoulder. Break yarn. *Next row* Place 31 (35, 41) stitches on hold for shoulder, rejoin yarn and cast on 1 stitch for selvage, work 37 collar stitches—38 stitches. Work even until collar measures 4" above shoulder, end with chart row 3.

*Shape top of collar*

*Begin short-row shaping: Row 1* (WS) P9, [p3tog, KPK] 7 times, p1. *Row 2* K1, p28, W&T. *Row 3* P8, [KPK, p3tog] 5 times, W&T. *Row 4* K1, p20, W&T. *Row 6* P8, [p3tog, KPK] 3 times, p1. *Row 6* K1, p12, W&T. *Row 7* [KPK, p3tog] 3 times, p1. Bind off all stitches purlwise.

## Sleeves

With larger needles, cast on 80 (88, 96) stitches. *Begin Charts A and B: Row 1* (RS) K1, work 12 (16, 20) stitches Chart A, 54 stitches Chart B, 12 (16, 20) stitches Chart A. Continue in patterns as established for 11 rows more. * Work 8-row increase in Chart A, work 8 rows even. Repeat from * 7 times more—144 (152, 160) stitches. Sleeve measures approximately 16½" from beginning.

*Shape cap*

Bind off 4 stitches at beginning of next 4 (6, 6) rows, 3 stitches at beginning of next 6 rows, 2 stitches at beginning of next 2 (2, 4) rows, 1 stitch at beginning of next 4 (10, 12) rows, 2 stitches at beginning of next 28 (24, 24) rows, 4 stitches at beginning of next 4 rows. Bind off remaining 30 (32, 34) stitches

## Finishing

Block pieces.

*Work all borders as follows*

With RS facing and smaller needles, pick up stitches as directed. [K 1 row, p 1 row] 4 times, k 1 row.

*Back*

Pick up and knit 110 (124, 135) stitches along lower edge.

*Left Front*

Begin at top of collar and pick up and knit 75 (78, 82) stitches to

beginning of curve at lower edge, 20 stitches around curve, 38 (43, 49) stitches to side edge.

*Right Front*

Place 3 markers for buttonholes along right front edge, using photo as guide to placement. Work band to correspond to left front, working buttonholes on row 3 by binding off 3 stitches at each marker; on row 4, cast on 3 stitches over bound-off stitches.

*Sleeve*

Pick up and knit 58 (62, 68) stitches along lower edge.

Join shoulders, using 3-needle bind-off as follows: join 31 (35, 41) stitches of first shoulder, bind off back neck stitches until 31 (35, 41) stitches remain, join 2nd shoulder. Sew colllar seam, including border. Sew collar to back neck, easing to fit. Sew on buttons. Set in sleeves. Sew side and sleeve seams, including borders.

## Stitch key

- ☐ Knit on RS, purl on WS
- ▨ Purl on RS, knit on WS
- ▨ *1/1 RC* Sl 1 to cn, hold to back, k1; k1 from cn.
- ▨ *1/1 LC* Sl 1 to cn, hold to front, k1; k1 from cn.
- ▨ *2/1 RPC* Sl 1 to cn, hold to back, k2; p1 from cn.
- ▨ *2/1 LPC* Sl 2 to cn, hold to front, p1; k2 from cn.
- ▨ *2/2 RC* Sl 2 to cn, hold to back, k2; k2 from cn.
- ▨ *2/2 LC* Sl 2 to cn, hold to front, k2; k2 from cn.
- ▨ *2/2 RPC* Sl 2 to cn, hold to back, k2; p2 from cn.
- ▨ *2/2 LPC* Sl 2 to cn, hold to front, p2; k2 from cn.
- ▨ *4/4 RC* Sl 4 to cn, hold to back, k4; k4 from cn.
- ▨ *4/4 LC* Sl 4 to cn, hold to front, k4; k4 from cn.

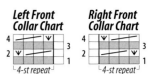

*Left Front Collar Chart* — 4-st repeat

*Right Front Collar Chart* — 4-st repeat

### Chart A

4-st repeat

- ▨ Purl on RS, knit on WS
- ⊻ KPK [K1, p1, k1] all in 1 st
- ╱ P3tog

On row 2 of the chart (a WS row), the KPK comes before the p3tog.

On row 4, the p3tog is worked on top of the KPK from row 2 and the KPK is worked on top of the p3tog.

### Chart B

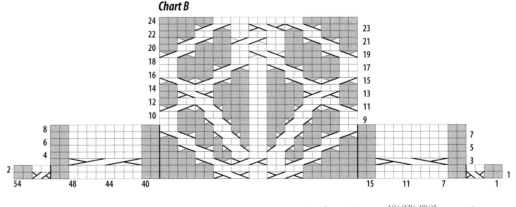

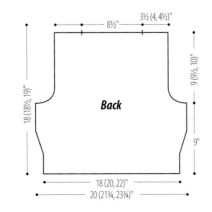

*Back*

18 (18½, 19)"
8½"
3½ (4, 4½)"
9 (9½, 10)"
9"
18 (20, 22)"
20 (21¾, 23¾)"

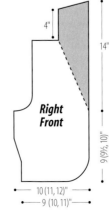

*Right Front*

4"
14"
9 (9½, 10)"
10 (11, 12)"
9 (10, 11)"

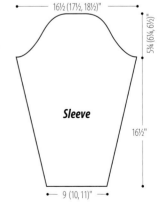

*Sleeve*

16½ (17½, 18½)"
5¾ (6¼, 6½)"
16½"
9 (10, 11)"

*A lightweight, felted-style wool-blend yarn and textural garter stitch work nicely together in this wearable, updated shape. The trim made from two strands of a tweedy wool ties it together.*

# snuggler sensation

**ADVANCED**

**OVERSIZED FIT**

**Sizes XS (S, M, L, 1X, 2X)**
**Shown in Medium**
A 41 (44¾, 48½, 52, 55, 58)"
B 20 (20½, 21, 21½, 22½, 23½)"
C 27½ (28, 29, 30½, 31½, 33)"

**10cm/4"**

16
9
• over garter stitch (knit every row), using size 8mm/US11 needles and MC

1 2 3 4 5 **6**

• **Super bulky weight**
MC • 550 (600, 660, 725, 790, 870) yds

1 2 **3** 4 5 6

• **Light weight**
CC • 345 (380, 415, 455, 495, 545) yds

• 5.5mm/US 9

• 4.5mm/US 7, 6mm/US 10, and 8mm/US 11, 74cm/29" long *or size to obtain gauge*

• One 36mm/1⅜"

• waste yarn

## Notes

**1** See *School*, page 94, for Make 1 (M1), SSK, loop cast-on, cable cast-on, 3-needle bind-off and grafting open stitches to finished edge. **2** Use 2 strands CC held together throughout. **3** Do not pick up short-row wraps.

## Wrap 1 stitch (W1), 2 stitches (W2) or 3 stitches (W3)

**Note:** Slip (sl) stitches purlwise.
*On a RS row* Sl 1, 2 or 3 stitches with yarn in back, bring yarn to front of work and sl stitch(es) back to left needle (1, 2 or 3 stitches wrapped).
*On a WS row* Sl 1, 2 or 3 stitches with yarn in front, bring yarn to back of work and sl stitch(es) back to left needle.

## Back

*Back band*
With size 6mm/US 10 needle and waste yarn, cast on 43 (47, 53, 57, 63, 69) stitches, using loop cast-on. **Work Tubular Edging** With 2 strands CC, [purl 1 row, knit 1 row] twice. Turn work so that purl side is facing (figure 1). Change to size 4.5mm/US 7 needle. *Next row* * Purl first stitch on left needle, then tip cast-on edge up and away from you and knit into first CC loop from first row (figure 2); repeat from * to last stitch on left needle, end p1, then pick up half-loop of CC at edge and knit it—86 (94, 106, 114, 126, 138) stitches. Remove waste yarn. *Begin Rib Pattern: Row 1* (RS) * P1, k1; repeat from * to end. Continue in Rib Pattern until piece measures 1¼" from beginning, end with a RS row. *Next row* (WS) K1, * k2tog; repeat from *, end k1—44 (48, 54, 58, 64, 70) stitches. Cut CC. Change to size 8mm/US 11 needle and MC. *Next row* (RS) Knit and decrease 10 (10, 12, 12, 14, 16) stitches evenly across—34 (38, 42, 46, 50, 54). Knit 11 (11, 11, 11, 13, 13) rows.
*Shape underarm*
**Increase Row** (RS) K2, M1, knit to last 2 stitches, M1, k2. Repeat Increase Row every 4th row twice more, then every other row twice—44 (48, 52, 56, 60, 64) stitches. Work 1 row even.
*Shape sleeves*
(**Note** Use cable cast-on for sleeve stitches.)
Cast on 4 stitches at beginning of next 16 rows, 4 (4, 4, 5, 6, 7) stitches at beginning of next 2 rows—116 (120, 124, 130, 136, 142) stitches. Knit 14 (16, 18, 20, 20, 22) rows.
*Shape shoulder and neck*
*Begin short-row shaping: Next 2 rows* Knit to last 7 stitches, W1, turn. *Next 2 rows* Knit to last 14 stitches, W1, turn. *Next 2 rows* Knit to last 21 (21, 21, 21, 21,

20) stitches, W1, turn. *Next 2 rows* Knit to last 28 (28, 28, 28, 28, 26) stitches, W1, turn. *Next 2 rows* Knit to last 34 (35, 35, 35, 35, 32) stitches, W1, turn. *Sizes 1X (2X) only: Next 2 rows* Knit to last 41 (38) stitches, W1, turn. *Size 2X only: Next 2 rows* Knit to last 44 stitches, W1, turn. *All Sizes: Shape neck: Row 1* (RS) K20 (21, 22, 24, 20, 20), join 2nd ball of yarn and bind off center 8 (8, 10, 12, 14, 14) stitches, k13 (13, 14, 15, 13, 13) more stitches, W1, turn. Working both sides at same time, work as follows: *Row 2* (WS) Knit 11 (11, 12, 13, 11, 11), SSK, k1; k1, k2tog, k11 (11, 12, 13, 11, 11), W1, turn. *Row 3* Knit 10 (10, 11, 12, 10, 10), k2tog, k1; k1, SSK, k4, W1, turn. *Row 4* K3, SSK, k1; k1, k2tog, k3, W1, turn. *Row 5* K2, k2tog, k1; k1, SSK, knit to end. *Row 6* Knit to last 3 stitches of first half, SSK, k1; on 2nd half, k1, k2tog, knit to end. Place remaining 49 (51, 52, 54, 56, 59) stitches each side on waste yarn.

## Left Front

*Front and neck band*
With size 6mm/US 10 needle and waste yarn, cast on 201 (213, 223, 235, 251, 263) stitches, using loop cast-on. Work Tubular Edging and rib as for back, end with a RS row. *Next row* (WS) K1, * k2tog; repeat from * to last stitch, k1—202 (214, 224, 236, 252, 264) stitches. Cut CC. Change to size 8mm/US 11 needle and MC.
*Shape front edge*
*Row 1* (RS) K1, [k2, k2tog] 2 (3, 3, 4, 5, 5) times, k1 (0, 2, 1, 0, 1), k2tog, W2, turn. *Row 2 and all WS rows* With size 8mm/US 11 needle, knit. *Row 3* Knit to band, [k2tog] twice, W2, turn. *Row 5* Knit to 2 stitches before band, [k2tog] 3 times, W2, turn. *Row 7* Knit to band, k2tog, W2, turn.
*Shape underarm*
*Row 9* K2, M1, knit to 2 stitches before band, [k2tog] twice, W2, turn. *Row 11* Knit to band, k2tog, W2, turn. *Row 13* K2, M1, knit to band, k2tog, W1, turn. *Row 15: Sizes XS, S, M, L* K2, M1, knit to band, k1, W1, turn. *Sizes 1X and 2X* Knit to band, k1, W1, turn. *All Sizes: Row 17* K2, M1, knit to 2 stitches before band, k2tog, k1, W1, turn. *Row 19* K2, M1, knit to band, k1, W2, turn. *Rows 21, 23, 25* K2, M1, knit to 2 stitches before band, [k2tog] twice, W2, turn—25 (27, 29, 31, 32, 33) MC stitches. *Sizes 1X and 2X: Row 27* K2, M1, knit to 2 stitches before band, [k2tog] twice, W2, turn—33 (34) MC stitches. Shape sleeve at beginning of RS rows and work cuff rows as for back, then shape shoulder at end of WS rows as follows: Knit to last 7 stitches, W1, turn. Continue working 7 fewer stitches at end of WS rows 3 (5, 6, 4, 4, 1) times, then 6 (6, 0, 8, 6, 6) fewer stitches 3 (1, 0, 2, 3, 7) times, AT SAME TIME, continue shaping left front edge as follows: *Row 27 (27, 27, 27, 29, 29)* Work to 2 stitches before band, [k2tog] twice, W2, turn. *Row 28 (28, 28, 28, 30, 30)* Knit. Repeat last 2 rows 5 times more.

*original yarn*
TAHKI•STACY CHARLES Tahki Fargo (wool blend; 50g; 60 yds) Oatmeal (MC)
TAHKI/STAHL Limbo (wool; 50g; 138 yds) Beige Tweed (CC)

T H E   B E S T   O F   K N I T T E R ' S

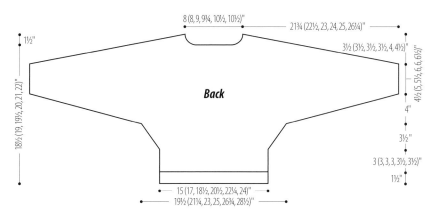

Back

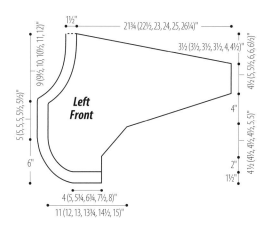

Left Front

*Shape neck*

**Row 1** (RS) Work to 5 stitches before band, [k2tog] twice, k3tog (1 MC stitch together with 2 band stitches), W3, turn. **Row 3** Work to 2 stitches before band, k2tog, k3tog, W2, turn. **Row 5** Work to 3 stitches before band, k2tog, k3tog, W2, turn. **Row 6** Knit. Repeat last 2 rows 5 (4, 5, 6, 7, 3) times more. * **Next row** (RS) Work to 3 stitches before band, k2tog, k3tog, W3, turn. **Next row** Knit. **Next row** Work to 2 stitches before band, k2tog, k3tog, W2, turn. **Next row** Knit. Repeat from * 2 (3, 3, 3, 3, 6) times more. **Next row** (RS) Work to 3 stitches before band, k2tog, k3tog, W3, turn. **Next row** Knit. **Next row** Work to 2 stitches before band, k2tog, k3tog, W3, turn. **Next row** Knit. Repeat last 2 rows twice more, omitting W3 on 2nd repeat (knit to end of row on last WS row). Place all stitches on waste yarn.

## Right Front

(**Note for working buttonhole:** Begin buttonhole 6 rows before neck shaping as follows: **Next row** (WS) Work to 2 stitches before band, [k2tog] twice, turn (omit W2). **Next row** Knit. **Next row** Knit to end, slip 4 stitches to waste yarn for buttonhole, turn. **Next row** Knit. **Next row** Knit to band, W2, turn. **Next row** Knit.)

Slip 10 (13, 15, 18, 21, 22) stitches from open end of band to a smaller spare needle. With size 11 needle and MC, work stitches from spare needle as follows: **Row 1** (RS) K1 (0, 2, 1, 0, 1), [k2tog, k2] 2 (3, 3, 4, 5, 5) times, k1. **Row 2** (WS) Knit to band, k2tog, W2, turn. **Row 3 and all following RS rows** Knit. **Row 4** Knit to band, [k2tog] twice, W2, turn (this row is equivalent to row 3 of left front). **Row 6** Knit to 2 stitches before band, [k2tog] 3 times, W2, turn. Continue working to correspond to left front, reversing shaping. Shape sleeve and shoulder at end of RS rows. Place remaining 18 (18, 20, 22, 24, 24) band stitches on waste yarn.

## Finishing

Block pieces lightly. Join front and back shoulders, using 3-needle bind-off. With MC, graft remaining band stitches to back neck.

*Cuffs*

With size 5.5mm/US 9 needles and waste yarn, cast on 18 (19, 20, 21, 21, 23) stitches, using loop cast-on. Work as for back band, ending with a WS row—19 (20, 21, 22, 22, 24) stitches. Cut CC. With MC, graft cuff stitches around lower edge of sleeves. Sew side and sleeve seams. Backstitch open loops of buttonhole, removing waste yarn. Sew on button.

# HOW TO:

## REVERSE ST ST TUBULAR EDGE

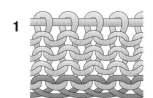

1

2

**Sizes S (M, L)**
*Blue color-way shown in Medium*
*Rust color-way shown in Small*
**A** 40 (48, 55)"
**B** 21 (23, 25)"
**C** 28 (30, 34)"

10cm/4"
46
23
• over Chart L

1 2 3 **4** 5 6

• *Medium weight*
**A, C, E** • 265 (350, 435) yds each
**B** • 420 (555, 695) yds
**D** • 330 (435, 545) yds
**F** • 175 (235, 290) yds

4.5mm/US 7, *or size to obtain
gauge*, 60cm/24" long

• 7 (8, 9) 22mm/⅞"

**&**

• stitch holders
• stitch markers

*original yarn*

CLASSIC ELITE Waterspun (wool; 50g; 138 yds) dark purple (A), moss (B), maroon (C), dark teal (D), grape (E), olive (F)
Reknit (as shown on pages 77 and 79) WESTMINSTER/NASHUA Creative Focus Worsted (wool, alpaca; 100g; 220 yds) chocolate (A), rust (B), cayenne, (C), espresso (D), copper (E), salmon (F)

Visit knittinguniverse.com to design your own color scheme with **Knitter's Paintbox**

*Charlene Schurch*

*This jacket is a masterpiece that is a joy to knit and great fun to wear. For all-season wearing, we've used a richly-toned wool yarn.*

# multicolor on the diagonal

## Notes

**1** See *School*, page 94, for knit cast-on (which is used throughout); M1 right-slanting (M1R) and left-slanting (M1L); and loop cast-on. **2** Jacket is worked in four sections which are sewn together. **3** Each section consists of blocks, half-blocks and "ribbons". Work 10 blocks and 2 half-blocks at yoke first, then work ribbons in 2 directions with blocks as foundation (see diagram). **4** Refer to Block and Ribbon charts to see what colors C1, C2, or C3 are for each block, half-block and ribbon. **5** Work tails in as you go. **6** Pick up stitches with RS of work facing.

### SECTION 1 (Right Back and 1/2 Sleeve)

**1** *Block 1*
**Note:** Slip (sl) stitches purlwise with yarn in front.
With C1, cast on 32 stitches. *Row 1* (WS) K3, [k2tog through back loop (tbl), k6] 3 times, k2tog tbl, k2, sl 1—28 stitches. *Row 2* With C2, knit to last stitch, sl 1. *Row 3* K1, p1, [p3tog, p4] 3 times, p3tog, p1, sl 1—20 stitches. *Row 4* With C1, knit to last stitch, sl 1. *Row 5* K1, [k3tog tbl, k2] 3 times, k3tog tbl, sl 1—12 stitches. *Row 6* With C2, knit to last stitch, sl 1. *Row 7* [P3tog tbl] 4 times. Cut yarn and run tail through remaining 4 stitches. Pull together tightly. Sew edges to form a square.
*Blocks 2–10*
With C1, cast on 12 stitches, then pick up and knit 8 stitches along seamed side of block just completed, cast on 12 stitches—32 stitches. Work as for Block 1.
*Half-block A*
With C1, cast on 8 stitches, then pick up and knit 8 stitches along seamed side of Block 10—16 stitches. *Row 1* (WS) K7, k2tog tbl, k6, sl 1—15 stitches. *Row 2* With C2, k2tog tbl, k12, sl 1—14 stitches. *Row 3* K2tog tbl, p4, p3tog, p4, sl 1—11 stitches. *Row 4* With C1, k2tog tbl, k8, sl 1—10 stitches. *Row 5* K2tog tbl, k2, k3tog tbl, k2, sl 1—7 stitches. *Row 6* With C2, k2tog tbl, k4, sl 1—6 stitches. *Row 7* K2tog tbl, p3tog tbl, * pass first stitch over 2nd stitch *, p1, repeat from * to *. Fasten off.
*Half-block B*
With C1, pick up and knit 8 stitches along side of Block 1 opposite to Block 2, then cast on 8 stitches—16 stitches. Work as for Half-block A.

**2** *Ribbon 1*
With C1, and holding blocks with Block 10 at right-hand side, pick up and knit 80 stitches evenly along Blocks 10–1. Work rows 2–16 of Chart A—65 stitches.

*Ribbon 2*
Work rows 1–16 of Chart A—49 stitches.
*Ribbon 3*
Work rows 1–16 of Chart A—33 stitches.
*Ribbon 4*
Place first 8 stitches on hold for neck, then work 16 rows of Chart A over remaining 25 stitches—9 stitches.
*Ribbon 5*
Work 8 rows of Chart B. Fasten off.

**3** *Ribbon 6*
Turn work upside down. With C1, pick up and knit 96 stitches along blocks from half-block to half-block. *Next row* (WS) K1, loop cast on 1 stitch, knit to last stitch, loop cast on 1 stitch, sl 1—98 stitches. Work rows 3–16 of Chart C—112 stitches.
*Ribbons 7–8 (7–10, 7–11)*
Work 16 rows of Chart C 2 (4, 5) times—144 (176, 192) stitches.
*Ribbon 12 (size L)*
Work 16 rows of Chart G—193 stitches.

### Section 1 (shown for size small only)

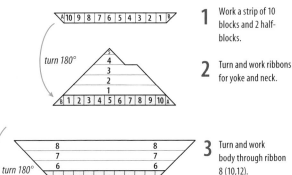

**1** Work a strip of 10 blocks and 2 half-blocks.

**2** Turn and work ribbons for yoke and neck.

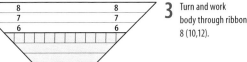

**3** Turn and work body through ribbon 8 (10,12).

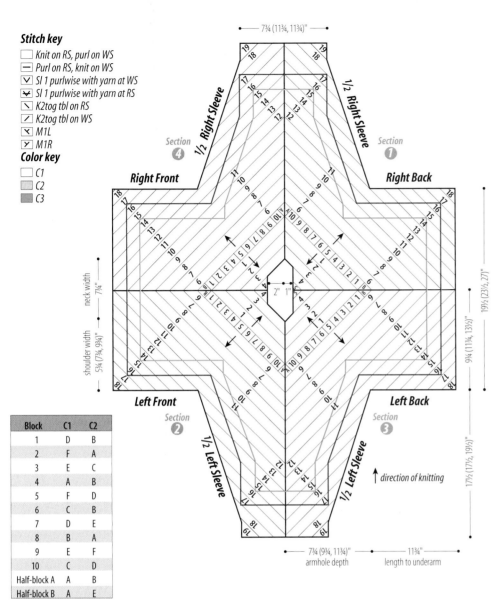

**Stitch key**
- ☐ Knit on RS, purl on WS
- ⊟ Purl on RS, knit on WS
- ☑ Sl 1 purlwise with yarn at WS
- ☑ Sl 1 purlwise with yarn at RS
- ☑ K2tog tbl on RS
- ☑ K2tog tbl on WS
- ☒ M1L
- ☒ M1R

**Color key**
- ☐ C1
- ▨ C2
- ▨ C3

7¾ (11¾, 11¾)"

½ Right Sleeve — Section ④

½ Right Sleeve — Section ①

**Right Front**

**Right Back**

neck width 7¾"

shoulder width 5¾ (7¾, 9¾)"

2" 1"

19½ (23½, 27)"

9¾ (11¾, 13½)"

**Left Front**

Section ②

**Left Back**

Section ③

½ Left Sleeve — Section ②

½ Left Sleeve — Section ③

↑ direction of knitting

17½ (17½, 19½)"

7¾ (9¾, 11¾)" armhole depth

11¾" length to underarm

| Block | C1 | C2 |
|---|---|---|
| 1 | D | B |
| 2 | F | A |
| 3 | E | C |
| 4 | A | B |
| 5 | F | D |
| 6 | C | B |
| 7 | D | E |
| 8 | B | A |
| 9 | E | F |
| 10 | C | D |
| Half-block A | A | B |
| Half-block B | A | E |

| Ribbon | C1 | C2 | C3 |
|---|---|---|---|
| 1 | A | F | C |
| 2 | B | D | E |
| 3 | D | C | F |
| 4 | E | A | C |
| 5 | C | B | — |
| 6 | D | E | B |
| 7 | C | F | D |
| 8 | B | E | A |
| 9 | E | D | F |
| 10 | A | C | B |
| 11 | D | A | B |
| 12 | E | F | C |
| 13 | C | B | A |
| 14 | B | D | A |
| 15 | E | C | D |
| 16 | A | B | E |
| 17 | D | B | C |
| 18 | C | D | A |
| 19 | B | E | F |
| Cuff & bands | B | D | C |

**Chart A**
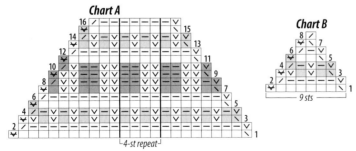
4-st repeat

**Chart B**
9 sts

**Chart C**
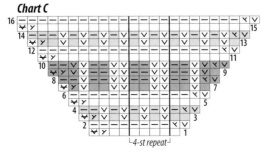
4-st repeat

**Chart G**
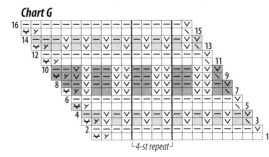
4-st repeat

**4** *Divide for back and sleeve*

*Next row* (RS) With C1 for Ribbon 9 (11, 13), [k2tog tbl] 0 (0, 1) time, then knit 79 (95, 94), sl 1 wyif, and place remaining 64 (80, 96) stitches on hold.

**Right Back**

*Ribbon 9 (size S)*

Work rows 2–16 of Chart D. Then with C1 for Ribbon 10, knit to last stitch, sl 1 wyif.

*Ribbon 10 (11, 13)*

Work rows 2–16 of Chart A—65 (81, 81) stitches.

*Ribbons 11–13 (12–15, 14–17)*

Work 16 rows of Chart A 3 (4, 4) times—17 stitches.

*Ribbon 14 (16, 18)*

Work 16 rows of Chart E. Fasten off.

*1/2 Right Sleeve*

Place 64 (80, 96) stitches from holder onto needle, ready to work a RS row.

## Sections (shown for size small only)

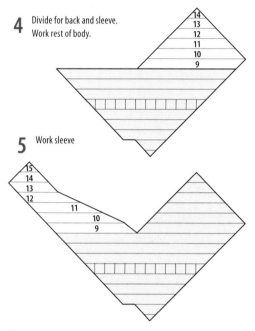

**4** Divide for back and sleeve.
Work rest of body.

**5** Work sleeve

**5** *Ribbon 9 (size S)*

Work rows 1–14 of Chart G.

*Next row* With C1, k3tog tbl, knit to last stitch, M1R, sl 1 wyif—64 stitches. *Next row* Knit to last stitch, sl 1 wyif.

*Ribbons 10-12 (11-14, 13-16)*

Work 16 rows of Chart F 3 (4, 4) times—40 (48, 64) stitches.

*Ribbon 13 (size S)*

Work rows 1–14 of chart F.

*Next row* With C1, k2tog tbl, knit to last stitch, M1R, sl 1 wyif—33 stitches. *Next row* Knit to last stitch, sl 1 wyif.

*Ribbon 15 (size M)*

*Next row* (RS) With C1, knit to last stitch, sl 1 wyif. Work rows 2–16 of Chart A—33 stitches.

*Ribbon 14 (size S) and Ribbon 16 (size M)*

Work 16 rows of Chart A—17 stitches.

*Ribbons 17–18 (size L)*

Work 16 rows of Chart H twice—16 stitches.

*Ribbon 15 (size S) and Ribbon 17 (size M)*

Work 16 rows of Chart E. Fasten off.

*Ribbon 19 (size L)*

*Next row* (RS) With C1, knit to last stitch, sl 1 wyif. Work rows 2–16 of Chart E. Fasten off.

**SECTION 2** (Left Front and 1/2 Sleeve)

Work as for Section 1 through Ribbon 3—33 stitches.

*Ribbon 4*

Place first 16 stitches on hold for neck, then work 16 rows of Chart E over remaining 17 stitches. Fasten off. Beginning with Ribbon 6, complete as for Section 1.

**SECTION 3** (Left Back and 1/2 Sleeve)

Work Blocks 1–10 as for Section 1.

*Half-block A*

With C1, pick up and knit 8 stitches along seamed side of Block 10, then cast on 8 stitches—16 stitches. Work as for Section 1.

*Half-block B*

With C1, cast on 8 stitches, then pick up and knit 8 stitches along side of Block 1 opposite Block 2. Work as for Section 1.

*Ribbon 1*

With C1, and holding blocks with Block 1 at right-hand side, pick up and knit 80 stitches evenly along Blocks 1–10. Work as for Section 1.

*Ribbons 2–3*

Work as for Section 1—33 stitches.

*Ribbon 4*

*Next row* (RS) Work Row 1 of Chart A over 25 stitches, place remaining 8 stitches on hold. Complete Chart A—9 stitches.

*Ribbon 5*

Work 8 rows of Chart B. Fasten off.

*Ribbons 6–8 (6–10, 6–11)*

Work as for Section 1—144 (176, 192) stitches.

*Ribbon 12 (size L)*

Work 16 rows of Chart D—192 stitches.

*Divide for back and sleeve*

*Next row* (RS) Place first 64 (80, 96) stitches on hold for sleeve—80 (96, 96) stitches remain.

**Left Back**

*Ribbon 9 (size S)*

Work 16 rows of Chart G—81 stitches.

*Ribbons 10–13 (size S)*

Work 16 rows of Chart A 4 times—17 stitches.

*Ribbon 14 (size S)*

Work 16 rows of Chart E. Fasten off.

*Ribbon 11 (size M) and Ribbon 13 (size L)*

*Next row* (RS) With C1, knit to last stitch, sl 1 wyif. Work rows 2–16 of Chart A—81 stitches.

*Ribbons 12–16 (size M) and 14–18 (size L)*

Work as for Back of Section 1.

**1/2 Left Sleeve**

Place 64 (80, 96) stitches from holder onto needle, ready to work a RS row.

*Ribbon 9 (size S)*

Work 16 rows of Chart D.

*Ribbons 10–13 (11–14, 13–16)*

Work 16 rows of Chart I four times—32 (48, 64) stitches.

*Ribbon 14 (size S)*

*Next row* (RS) With C1, knit to last stitch, sl 1 wyif. Work rows 2–16 of Chart A—17 stitches.

*Ribbon 15 (size S)*

Work 16 rows of Chart E. Fasten off.

*Ribbons 15–17 (size M)*

Work as for Sleeve of Section 1.

*Ribbon 17 (size L)*

*Next row* (RS) With C1, knit to last stitch, sl 1. Work rows 2–16 of Chart J—41 stitches.

*Ribbon 18 (size L)*

Work 16 rows of Chart J—17 stitches.

*Ribbon 19 (size L)*

Work 16 rows of Chart E. Fasten off.

**SECTION 4** (Right Front and 1/2 Sleeve)

Work as for Section 3 through Ribbon 3—33 stitches.

*Ribbon 4*

With C1, work Row 1 of Chart E over 17 stitches, place remaining 16 stitches on hold for neck. Complete Chart E. Beginning with Ribbon 6, complete as for Section 3.

**Finishing**

**Note:** When sewing seams, work ½ stitch in from edge so that half of each slip stitch shows.

Sew fronts to backs at top of sleeves.

*Cuff bands*

With C1, pick up and knit 34 (50, 50) stitches along sleeve cuff. Work 14 rows of Chart K. Bind off knitwise. Sew back, side and sleeve seams.

*Lower-edge band*

With C1, pick up and knit 160 (192, 224) stitches along lower edge.

*Next row* (WS) K2, loop cast on 1 stitch (increase 1), [k4, increase 1] 39 (47, 55) times, k2—200 (240, 280) stitches. Work 16 rows of Chart L.

*Next row* (RS) With C1, knit to last stitch, sl 1. Bind off knitwise.

**Chart D**

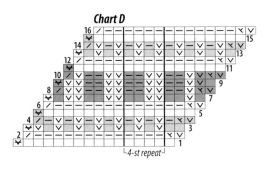

4-st repeat

**Chart E**

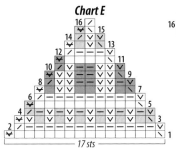

17 sts

**Chart F**

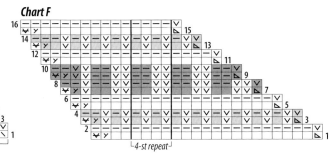

4-st repeat

**Chart H**

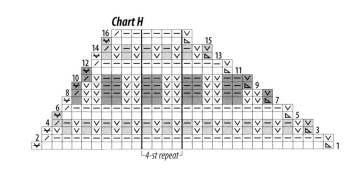

4-st repeat

**Chart I**

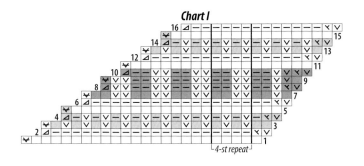

4-st repeat

*Front and neckband*

With C1, pick up and knit 82 (90, 98) stitches along right front, place marker (pm), 8 stitches to holder, k16 from front neck holder, and 8 stitches from back neck holder, pick up and knit 26 stitches along back neck placing a marker after 13th stitch, k8 from back neck holder, and 16 stitches from front neck holder, pick up and knit 8 stitches along left front neck, pm, then 82 (90, 98) stitches along left front edge—254 (270, 286) stitches.

*Row 1* (WS) Knit to first marker, slip marker (sm), loop cast on 1 stitch (increase 1), pm, knit to last marker, sm, increase 1, pm, knit to end—256 (272, 288) stitches. *Row 2* With C2, * k1, sl 1; repeat from * to marker, sm, M1, k1, M1, sm, * sl 1, k1; repeat from * to 1 stitch before marker, sl 1, sm, k2tog, * sl 1, k1; repeat from * to 1 stitch before marker, sl 1, sm, M1, k1, M1, sm, * sl 1, k1; repeat from * to end—259 (275, 291) stitches. *Row 3* K1, * sl 1, k1; repeat from * to end. *Row 4* With C1, knit to marker, sm, [k1, M1] twice, k1, sm, knit to marker, sm, M1, knit to marker, sm, [k1, M1] twice, k1, sm, knit to end—264 (280, 296) stitches. *Row 5* Knit. *Row 6* With C3, * k2, sl 2; repeat from * to 2 stitches before marker, k2, sl 2, M1, k1, M1, sl 2, * k2, sl 2; repeat from * to 2 stitches after 2nd-to-last marker, M1, k1, M1, * sl 2, k2; repeat from * to end—268 (284, 300) stitches. *Row 7* * K2, sl 2; repeat from * to 2 stitches after marker, k3, * sl 2, k2; repeat from * to 2nd-to-last marker, sl 2, k3, * sl 2, k2; repeat from * to end. *Row 8* (buttonhole row) Begin row for each size as follows: *Size S,* K1, p1; *Size M,* K1, p1, sl 2, p2, sl 2, yo, p2tog; *Size L,* K1, p1, sl 2, yo, p2tog; then *ALL Sizes,* * [sl 2, p2] twice, sl 2, yo, p2tog; repeat from * 5 (5, 6) times more, [sl 2, p2] twice, sl 2, p1, M1, yo, p2tog, M1, sl 2, * p2, sl 2; repeat from * to 2 stitches after 2nd-to-last marker, p1, [M1, p1] twice, sl 2, * p2, sl 2; repeat from *, end p1, k1—272 (288, 304) stitches. *Row 9* * K2, sl 2; repeat from * to 2 stitches after marker, k5, * sl 2, k2; repeat from * to 2nd-to-last marker, sl 2, k5, * sl 2, k2; repeat from * to end. *Row 10* With C1, knit to marker, k4, M1, k1, M1, k4, knit to 1 stitch before center marker, k2tog removing marker, knit to next marker, k4, M1, k1, M1, knit to end—275 (291, 307) stitches. *Row 11* Knit. *Row 12* With C2, k2, * sl 1, k1; repeat from * to 4 stitches after marker, sl 1, M1, k1, M1, * sl 1, k1; repeat from * to 4 stitches after 2nd-to-last marker, sl 1, M1, k1, M1, * sl 1, k1; repeat from * to last 3 sts, sl 1, k2—279 (295, 311) stitches. *Row 13* K2, * sl 1, k1; repeat from * to last 3 stitches, sl 1, k2. *Row 14* With C1, [knit to marker, k6, M1, k1, M1, k6] twice, knit to end—283 (299, 315) stitches. Bind off knitwise. Sew on buttons.

**Chart J**

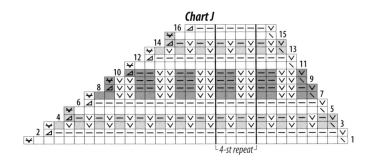

4-st repeat

**Chart K**

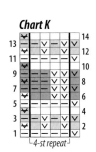

4-st repeat

**Chart L**

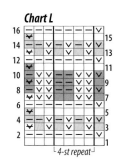

4-st repeat

**Stitch key**

☐ Knit on RS, purl on WS
— Purl on RS, knit on WS
∨ Sl 1 purlwise with warn at WS
❤ Sl 1 purlwise with yarn at RS
◣ K2tog tbl on RS
◢ K2tog tbl on WS
◣ K3 tog tbl on RS
◢ K3 tog tbl on WS
◄ M1L
► M1R

# warm & wonderful

*Linda Cyr*

Here is a season-spanning coat that will take you from fall through winter. Worked in easy knit and purl stitches, it's extra warm in a mohair blend and llama/wool. Stylish buttons and a neat bias trim add to its beauty.

# nine-to-five

**INTERMEDIATE**

**LOOSE FIT**

**Sizes XS (S, M, L, 1X)**
**Shown in Medium**

*A* 46 (48½, 51½, 54½, 57½)"
*B* 28 (28, 29, 29, 29¾)"
*C* 27½ (28, 30, 32, 33½)"

**10cm/4"**

18
11
• over Chart Patterns,
using larger needles and 1 strand
each A and B held together

1 2 3 4 **5** 6
• Bulky weight
*A & B* • 1025 (1065, 1195, 1270,
1385) yds each
*C* • 95 yds

• 4mm/US 6 and 6mm/US 10,
or size to obtain gauge

• five 25mm/1"

• stitch holders
• stitch markers

**original yarn**
CLASSIC ELITE Montera (llama, wool;
100g; 127 yds) camel (A); La Gran
(mohair, wool, nylon; 40g; 90 yds) otter
(B); Tapestry (wool blend; 50g; 95 yds)
black (C)

**Notes** *1* See *School*, page 94, for Make 1 (M1) and SSK. *2* Coat is worked with 1 strand each A and B held together throughout. Use 1 strand of C for bindings. *3* Begin Chart Patterns with first stitch of chart; last stitch of chart will not always correspond to last stitch of row. *4* Keep 1 stitch at each edge in stockinette stitch (St st) (knit on RS, purl on WS) for selvage; work all increases and decreases inside selvage stitches.

## Back

With larger needles and 1 strand A and B held together, cast on 52 (56, 60, 64, 68) stitches. *Begin Chart A: Row 1* (RS) K1 (selvage stitch), work Chart A to last stitch, k1 (selvage stitch). Continue in chart pattern as established, AT SAME TIME, increase 1 stitch each side (working increases into pattern) every RS row 6 times—64 (68, 72, 76, 80) stitches. Work even until 24 rows of Chart A have been worked. *Next row* (RS) K1, purl to last stitch, k1. *Next row* P1, knit to last stitch, p1. Work Chart B for 24 rows. *Next row* (RS) K1, purl to last stitch, k1. *Next row* P1, knit to last stitch, p1. Work Chart C for 24 rows. *Next row* (RS) K1, purl to last stitch, k1. *Next row* P1, knit to last stitch, p1. Piece measures approximately 17½" from beginning.

*Shape armholes*
Work Chart D, AT SAME TIME, bind off 2 stitches at beginning of next 2 rows. Work 2 rows even. Decrease 1 stitch each side every RS row twice—56 (60, 64, 68, 72). Work even until 24 rows of Chart D have been completed. *Next row* (RS) K1, purl to last stitch, k1. *Next row* P1, knit to last stitch, p1. Work Chart E for 18 (18, 22, 22, 26) rows. Armhole measures approximately 9¾ (9¾, 10¾, 10¾, 11½)".

*Shape shoulders*
Bind off 9 (10, 10, 11, 12) stitches at beginning of next 2 rows, 8 (9, 10, 10, 11) stitches at beginning of next 2 rows. Bind off remaining 22 (22, 24, 26, 26) stitches.

## Pocket linings (make 2)
With larger needles and 1 strand A and B held together, cast on 22 stitches. Work in St st for 8½". Place stitches on a holder.

## Left Front
With larger needles and 1 strand A and B held together, cast on 30 (32, 34, 36, 38) stitches. Work in chart patterns and work increases at side edge (beginning of RS rows) as for back—36 (38, 40, 42, 44) stitches. Work even until 18 rows of Chart B have been completed. Piece measures approximately 9¾" from beginning.

*Join pocket lining*
*Next row* (RS) Work 5 (7, 7, 9, 11) stitches, bind off 22 stitches, work to end.

*Next row* (WS) Work to bound-off stitches, then with WS of lining facing, work across 22 stitches of pocket lining, work to end. Work even until piece measures same length as back to underarm. Shape armhole at side edge as for back—32 (34, 36, 38, 40) stitches. Work even until 2 rows of Chart E have been completed. Armhole measures approximately 6".

*Shape neck*
*Next row* (RS) Work to last 3 stitches, k2tog, k1 (neck edge). Work 1 (1, 3, 3, 5) rows even. Decrease 1 stitch at neck edge on next row. Work 2 rows even. Bind off 7 (7, 7, 8, 7) stitches at beginning of next row, then 2 stitches every other row twice. Decrease 1 stitch at neck edge on next row, then every other row 1 (1, 2, 2, 3) times more—17 (19, 20, 21, 23) stitches. Work 3 rows even. Shape shoulder by binding off at beginning of RS rows 9 (10, 10, 11, 12) stitches once, 8 (9, 10, 10, 11) stitches once. Place markers for 5 buttons along left front edge, with the first at beginning of neck shaping, the last 6" from lower edge and 3 others spaced evenly between.

## Right Front
(*Note* Work buttonholes to correspond to button markers on left front as follows: *On a RS row* Work 3 stitches, bind off 2 stitches, work to end. On next row, cast on 2 stitches over bound-off stitches.)
Work as for left front to pocket lining joining, reversing lower edge shaping by working increases at end of RS rows.

*Join pocket lining*
*Next row* (RS) Work 9 (9, 11, 11, 11) stitches, bind off 22 stitches, work to end. Continue as for left front until piece measures same length as back to underarm, end with a RS row. Shape armhole at side edge as for back—32 (34, 36, 38, 40) stitches. Work even until same length as left front to neck shaping.

*Shape neck*
*Next row* (RS) K1, SSK, work to end. Work 1 (1, 3, 3, 5) rows even. Decrease 1 stitch at neck edge on next row. Work 1 row even. Bind off 7 (7, 7, 8, 7) stitches at beginning of next row, then 2 stitches every other row twice. Work 1 row even. Decrease 1 stitch at neck edge on next row, then every other row 1 (1, 2, 2, 3) times more—17 (19, 20, 21, 23) stitches. Work 4 rows even. Shape shoulder by binding off at beginning of WS rows 9 (10, 10, 11, 12) stitches once, 8 (9, 10, 10, 11) stitches once.

## Sleeves
With larger needles and 1 strand each A and B held together, cast on 34 (34, 36, 36, 38) stitches. Work Chart F for 14 rows. Work Chart A for 10 rows. Continue working Chart A, AT SAME TIME, increase 1 stitch each side (working increases into pattern) on next row, then every 4th row 2 (2, 6, 3, 5) times, every 6th row 6 (6, 4, 7, 6)

times—52 (52, 58, 58, 62) stitches. Work even until piece measures 16 (16, 17, 18, 18½)" from beginning, end with a WS row.

*Shape cap*

Bind off 2 stitches at beginning of next 2 rows. Decrease 1 stitch each side every row 5 (5, 5, 5, 7) times, then every other row 2 (2, 2, 2, 3) times, then every row 3 (3, 5, 5, 3) times. Bind off 2 stitches at beginning of next 0 (0, 2, 2, 0) rows, 3 stitches at beginning of next 4 (4, 2, 2, 4) rows. Bind off remaining 16 (16, 20, 20, 20) stitches.

### Finishing

Block pieces. Sew shoulders. Sew pocket linings to WS.

### Collar

With RS facing, larger needles and 1 strand each A and B, begin at right front neck edge, pick up and knit 51 (51, 57, 59, 63) stitches evenly around neck edge. Work row 2 of Chart F. Continue working Chart F, AT SAME TIME, work increases on next RS row as follows: Increase 1 st in first and last stitch of row and work 1 pair of increase stitches at each shoulder seam—57 (57, 63, 65, 69) stitches. [Work 3 rows even, work increase row] twice—69 (69, 75, 77, 81) stitches. Work 3 rows even. Bind off.

### Bias binding

With smaller needles and 1 strand C, cast on 8 stitches. ***Begin Bias Pattern: Row 1*** (RS) K1, M1, k5, k2tog. ***Row 2*** Purl. Repeat rows 1 and 2 until piece fits along lower edge of back, including 2¾" curved edges. Fold binding in half and pin along lower edge of back, enclosing cast-on edge and easing around shaped edges. Sew in place. In same way, work binding and sew along lower edge of right front (including curved edge), along right front edge, along collar edge, then along left front to correspond to right front. Work binding and sew to lower edges of each sleeve. Set in sleeves. Sew sleeve seams, reversing seam at last 3" for fold-back cuff. Sew side seams, leaving curved edges open and tucking ends of binding into seams. Sew on buttons.

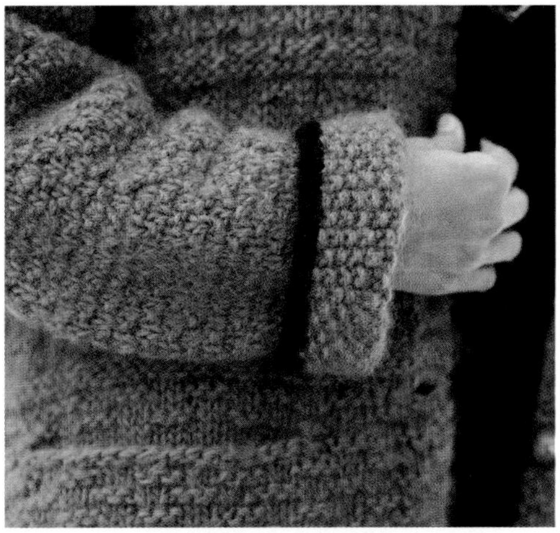

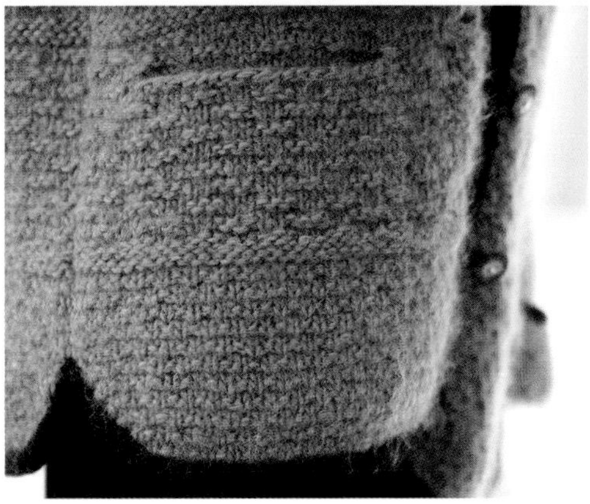

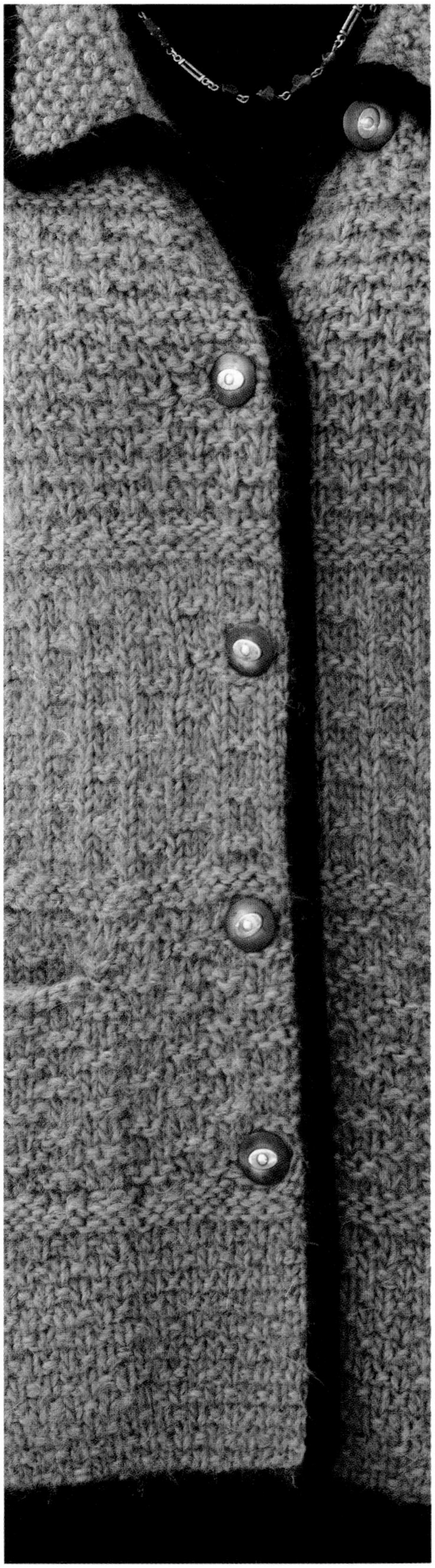

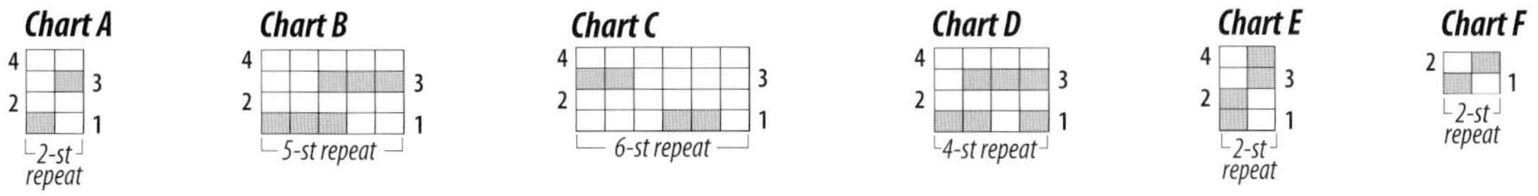
Chart A
4
3
2
1
2-st repeat
Chart B
5-st repeat
Chart C
6-st repeat
Chart D
4-st repeat
Chart E
2-st repeat
Chart F
2-st repeat

**Stitch key**

- ☐ *Knit on RS, purl on WS*
- ▒ *Purl on RS, knit on WS*

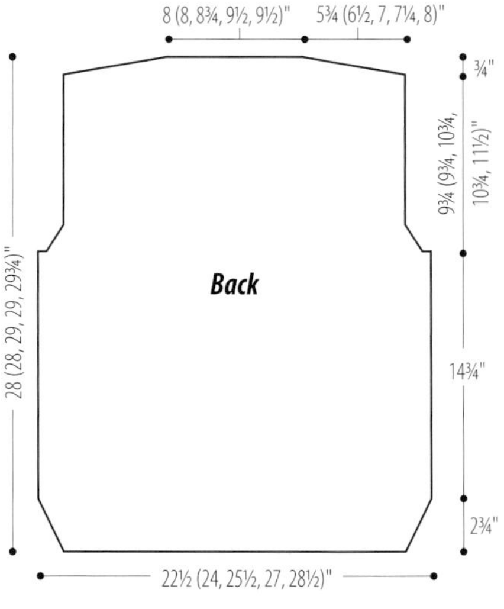
8 (8, 8¾, 9½, 9½)"
5¾ (6½, 7, 7¼, 8)"
¾"
9¾ (9¾, 10¾, 10¾, 11½)"
28 (28, 29, 29, 29¾)"
Back
14¾"
2¾"
22½ (24, 25½, 27, 28½)"

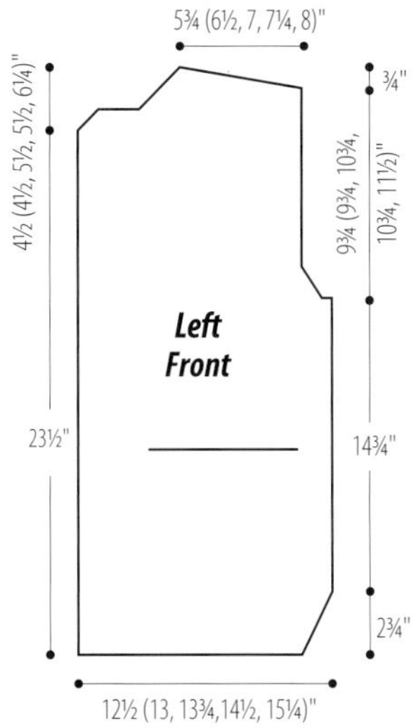
5¾ (6½, 7, 7¼, 8)"
4½ (4½, 5½, 5½, 6¼)"
¾"
9¾ (9¾, 10¾, 10¾, 11½)"
Left Front
23½"
14¾"
2¾"
12½ (13, 13¾, 14½, 15¼)"

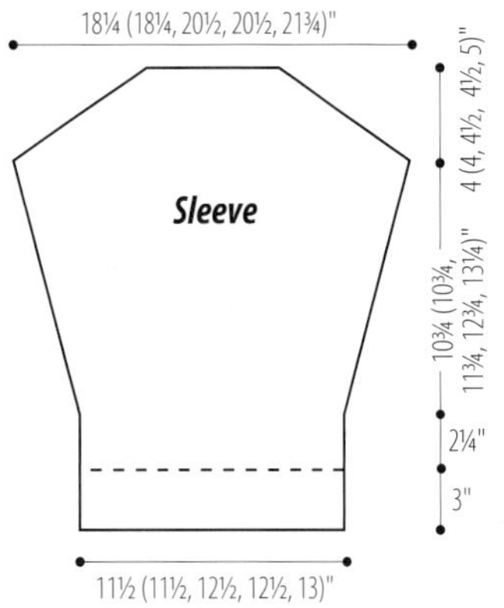
18¼ (18¼, 20½, 20½, 21¾)"
4 (4, 4½, 4½, 5)"
Sleeve
10¾ (10¾, 11¾, 12¾, 13¼)"
2¼"
3"
11½ (11½, 12½, 12½, 13)"

Barbara Venishnick

A sophisticated look is yours to behold and to wear. If you want fun techniques using special hand-dyed yarns, this coat is one to try. The mohair-blend bouclé is paired with a rich alpaca/wool blend. The center hook closure leaves uninterrupted lines that are extremely flattering.

# the cuddle coat

**INTERMEDIATE**

**LOOSE FIT**

**Sizes S (M, L, 1X)**
**Shown in Small**
**A** 44 (48¾, 52¾, 57)"
**B** 28 (29, 30, 30)"
**C** 27½ (28¾, 29½, 30¾)"

**10cm/4"**
23
22

• over Chart Pattern,
using 5.5mm/US 9 needles

1 2 3 **4** 5 6

• **Medium weight**
MC • 1650 (1825, 2000, 2110) yds
CC • 825 (915, 1000, 1060) yds

• 3.75mm/US 5, 4mm/US 6, 5.5mm/
US 9 or size to obtain gauge

• 4mm/US 6, 74cm/29" long

**&**

• stitch markers
• 3 large hook-and-eye closures

**original yarn**

CHERRY TREE HILL FARM Alpaca
(alpaca blend; 224g; 500 yds)
Chocolate (MC)
Froth (mohair, wool, nylon; 224g; 500
yds) Martha's Vineyard (CC)

## Notes

**1** See *School*, page 94 for SSK. **2** Carry unused yarn loosely along WS until it's needed again.

## Back

With size 4mm/US 6 needles and MC, cast on 121 (133, 145, 157) stitches. ***Work welt: Rows 1, 3 and 5*** (RS) Purl. ***Rows 2, 4*** Knit. ***Row 6*** Purl. Change to size 5.5mm/US 9 needles. Work in chart pattern until piece measures 25 (26, 27, 27)" from beginning, end with a WS row.

*Shape shoulders*

Bind off 5 (5, 5, 6) stitches at beginning of next 18 (10, 2, 10) rows, 0 (6, 6, 7) stitches at beginning of next 0 (8, 16, 8) rows. Bind off remaining 31 (35, 39, 41) stitches.

## Right Front

With size 4mm/US 6 needles and MC, cast on 61 (67, 73, 79) stitches. Work as for back until piece measures 17" from beginning, end with a WS row.

*Shape V-neck*

***Next row*** (RS) K1, SSK, work to end. Continue to decrease 1 stitch at neck edge every other row 2 (3, 4, 6) times more, then every 4th row 13 (14, 15, 14) times, AT SAME TIME, when piece measures same length as back to shoulder, shape shoulder at beginning of WS rows as for back.

## Left Front

Work as for right front, reversing shaping. Work neck decreases as follows: On a RS row, work to last 3 stitches, k2tog, k1. Shape shoulder at beginning of RS rows.

## Sleeves

With size 4mm/US 6 needles and MC, cast on 55 stitches. Work 6-row welt as for back, increasing 18 stitches evenly across last row—73 stitches. Change to size 5.5mm/US 9 needles. Work in chart pattern, AT SAME TIME, increase 1 stitch each side (working increases into pattern), on 5th row, then every 4th row 3 (12, 18, 18) times, then every 6th row 12 (6, 2, 2) times—105 (111, 115, 115) stitches. Work even until piece measures 17" from beginning, end with a WS row. Bind off.

## Finishing

Block pieces. Place a marker on each side of back 7 (8, 9, 9)" up from lower edge.

*Right pocket lining*

With RS of back facing, size 3.75mm/US 5 needles and MC, begin at right edge marker and pick up and knit 1 stitch in each of next 35 rows. ***Rows 1 and 3*** (WS) Purl. ***Row 2*** Knit. ***Row 4*** K1, increase 1 stitch in next stitch, knit to last 3 stitches, k2tog, k1. Repeat these 4 rows 10 times more, then work rows 1 and 2 once. Bind off.

*Left pocket lining*

With RS of back facing, size 3.75mm/US 5 needles and MC, begin 35 rows above left edge marker and pick up and knit 1 stitch in each of next 35 rows, ending at marker. Work as for right pocket lining, except work row 4 as follows: K1, SSK, knit to last 2 stitches, increase 1 stitch in next stitch, k1.

*Work welts*

(**Note:** Work welts as follows: [K 1 row, p 1 row] twice. Bind off knitwise.)

*Right shoulder welt*

With RS of back facing, size 4mm/US 6 needles and MC, pick up and knit 45 (49, 53, 58) stitches along right shoulder. Work welt. Cut yarn, leaving a 24–27" tail.

*Left shoulder welt*

Work as for right shoulder, except pick up stitches along left shoulder.

*Join shoulders*

Pin welt back out of the way. Then, with WS of right front and back together, sew shoulder seam along welt pick-up row. Unpin welt and allow it to curl naturally over seam. Tack down welt with long tail left after bind-off. Sew left shoulder in same way.

*Right side welt*

Place markers 9½ (10, 10½, 10½)" down from shoulder on front and back for armholes. With RS facing, circular needle and MC, begin at back armhole marker and pick up and knit 1 stitch in every row to shoulder, then continue picking up 1 stitch in every row past front armhole marker down to lower edge of front. Work welt.

*Left side welt*

Work as for right side, except begin picking up stitches at lower edge of left front and down to back marker. Sew sleeves between armhole markers, working same as for shoulders. Do not tack down welt after joining. Sew sleeve seams. Sew side seams in same way, leaving 35 pocket lining stitches free. Sew pocket linings to WS of fronts.

## Collar

(**Note:** For ease in working, mark RS of collar.)

With size 5.5mm/US 9 needles and MC, cast on 29 stitches. Knit 5 rows. Continue in garter stitch (knit every row) and stripe pattern as follows: * 2 rows CC, 6 rows MC; repeat from * 13 times more. Continue in stripe pattern, AT SAME TIME, increase 1 stitch each side on next row, then every other row 3 times more, then every 4th row 6 times—49 stitches. Work 1 row even. Work 8 rows of stripe pattern 23 (25, 28, 28) times, then work rows 1–4 once. Continue in stripe pattern, decreasing 1 stitch each side on next row, then every 4th row 5 times more, then every other row 4 times. Work

CHERRY TREE HILL FARM Alpaca (alpaca blend; 224g; 500 yds) Chocolate (MC) Froth (mohair, wool, nylon; 224g; 500 yds) Martha's Vineyard (CC)

1 row even. [Knit 6 rows MC, knit 2 rows CC] 14 times. With MC, knit 5 rows. Bind off all stitches knitwise. With RS of collar facing RS of coat, pin collar along front edges and back neck, with straight edges of collar along straight front edges, and shaped edges along neck. Slightly stretch narrow section along straight edge of fronts if necessary and gather extra ease at each shoulder side of back neck. Sew collar in place. Fold collar in half to WS with ¼" overlap to inside and sew in place. Tack collar back to coat fronts at lower edge. Sew 3 hook-and-eye closures to inside of coat at collar seam, with the first at beginning of neck shaping, the last approximately 10" from lower edge, and one placed evenly between.

CHERRY TREE HILL FARM Alpaca (alpaca blend; 224g; 500 yds) Chocolate (MC) Froth (mohair, wool, nylon; 224g; 500 yds) Java (CC)

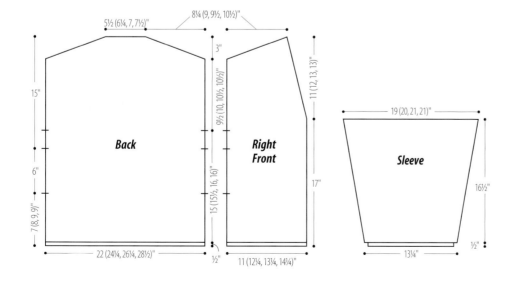

**Chart Pattern**

6-st repeat

**Stitch key**
- ☐ Knit on RS, purl on WS
- ▬ Knit on WS

**Color key**
- ▨ MC
- ☐ CC

*Wearing this classic jacket announces to the world that you are first and foremost a knitter! The wool/mohair yarn turned out to be the perfect fiber for fulling.*

# felted knitter's surprise

**INTERMEDIATE**

**OVERSIZED FIT**

**Sizes S (M, L, 1X)**
**Shown in Small**
A 44 (48, 52, 56)"
B 26 (27, 28, 29)"
C 28½ (30, 31½, 33½)"

**10cm/4"**

22
18
• *before fulling: in stockinette stitch (knit on RS, purl on WS), using smaller needles and MC*

1 2 3 **4** 5 6

• *Medium weight*
MC • 1520 (1685, 1865, 2065) yds
C • 245 (245, 245, 245) yds

1 2 3 4 **5** 6

• *Bulky weight*
A • 220 (220, 220, 220) yds
B • 125 (125, 125, 125) yds

5mm/US 8 and 6mm/US 10,
*or size to obtain gauge*

• *five 22mm/⅞"*

• stitch holders
• tailor's chalk

**Note** See *School*, page 94 for SSK.

**Gauge swatch**

(Make 2; use for pocket linings)

Get familiar with the fulling process and obtain a close estimate of gauge and texture after fulling by working a gauge swatch as follows: With smaller needles and MC, cast on 34 stitches. Work in stockinette stitch (St st) for 46 rows. Bind off. Piece should measure approximately 7½" wide and 8½" long.

**Fulling**

To protect your washer from excess fiber, place piece to be fulled into a zippered pillow protector or fine mesh bag. Set washer for hot wash, low water level and maximum agitation. (Using the rinse and spin cycles is not recommended as they may set permanent creases.) Add a small amount of mild detergent, and two old towels (non-shedding) or pairs of jeans for abrasion. Check on the progress every few minutes. Every time you check the progress, pull the garment into shape. Reset the washer to continue agitation if necessary. When you are happy with the size, remove from washer. Rinse thoroughly in warm water. Roll in towels to remove as much water as possible. Pull into shape. Swatch should measure 6¾" wide and 7½" long. If it doesn't, begin above process again, checking every few minutes until dimensions are achieved. Record details of process for fulling of jacket. Pin damp pieces to finished dimensions, steam block and let dry.

**Back**

With smaller needles and MC, cast on 96 (106, 116, 126) stitches. Work in St st, AT SAME TIME, increase 1 stitch each side every other row 3 times, every 4th row once—104 (114, 124, 134) stitches. Work even until piece measures 4" from beginning, end with a WS row. Cast on 3 stitches at beginning of next 2 rows—110 (120, 130, 140) stitches. Work even until piece measures 17 (17½, 18½, 19)" from beginning, end with a WS row.

*Shape armholes*

Bind off 4 stitches at beginning of next 2 rows. Decrease 1 stitch each side on next row, then every other row once more, every 4th row twice—94 (104, 114, 124) stitches. Work even until armhole measures 11 (11½, 12, 12½)", end with a WS row. Mark center 22 (24, 26, 28) stitches.

*Shape shoulders and neck*

Bind off 8 (9, 10, 11) stitches at beginning of next 8 rows, AT SAME TIME, after 2 rows have been worked, bind off center marked stitches for neck and working both sides at same time, bind off from each neck edge 4 stitches once.

**Pocket extensions** (Make 2)

With smaller needles and MC, cast on 34 stitches. Work in St st for 6 rows. Place stitches on hold.

**Left Front**

With smaller needles and MC, cast on 48 (53, 58, 63) stitches. Work as for back until piece measures 4" from beginning, end with a WS row—56 (61, 66, 71) stitches. Cast on 3 stitches at beginning of next (RS) row—59 (64, 69, 74) stitches. Work even until piece measures 9½ (10, 10½, 11)" from beginning, end with a WS row.

*Join pocket extension*

**Next row** (RS) K13 (16, 19, 22), bind off 34 stitches, knit to end. **Next row** (WS) P12 (14, 16, 18), then with WS facing, p34 stitches of pocket extension, purl to end. Work even until piece measures same length as back to underarm. Shape armhole at beginning of RS rows as for back—51 (56, 61, 66) stitches. Work even until armhole measures 7½ (8, 8½, 9)", end with a WS row.

*Shape neck*

**Decrease Row** (RS) Knit to last 2 stitches, k2tog. Work 3 rows even. Repeat decrease row on next row, then every other row twice more. **Next row** (WS) Bind off 6 (7, 8, 9) stitches, work to end. Continue to bind off at beginning of WS rows 5 stitches once, 2 stitches once. Repeat decrease row on next row, then every other row once more—32 (36, 40, 44) stitches. Work even until armhole measures same length as back to shoulder, end with a WS row.

*Shape shoulder*

Bind off 8 (9, 10, 11) sts at beginning of every RS row 4 times.

**Right Front**

Work as for left front until piece measures 4" from beginning, end with a RS row—56 (61, 66, 71) stitches. Cast on 3 stitches at beginning of next (WS) row—59 (64, 69, 74) stitches. Work even until piece measures 9½ (10, 10½, 11)" from beginning, end with a WS row.

*Join pocket extension*

**Next row** (RS) K12 (14, 16, 18), bind off 34 stitches, knit to end. **Next row** (WS) P13 (16, 19, 22), then with WS facing, p34 stitches of pocket extension, purl to end. Work even until piece measures same length as back to underarm, end with a RS row. Shape armhole at beginning of WS row and end of RS rows as for back—51 (56, 61, 66) stitches. Work even until armhole measures 7½ (8, 8½, 9)", end with a WS row.

*original yarn*

BROWN SHEEP COMPANY Lamb's Pride Worsted (wool; mohair; 113g; 190 yds) charcoal heather (MC) Lamb's Pride Superwash Bulky (wool; 100g; 110 yds) black (A) Lamb's Pride Bulky (wool; mohair; 113g; 125 yds) creme (B) Nature Spun Worsted (wool; 100g; 245 yds) gray heather (C)

## Shape neck
**Decrease Row** (RS) SSK, knit to end. Work 3 rows even. Repeat Decrease Row on next row, then every other row twice more. Work 1 row even. **Next row** (RS) Bind off 6 (7, 8, 9) stitches, work to end. Continue to bind off at beginning of RS rows 5 stitches once, 2 stitches once. Repeat Decrease Row every other row twice—32 (36, 40, 44) stitches. Work even until armhole measures same length as back to shoulder, end with a RS row.

## Shape shoulder
Bind off at beginning of WS rows 8 (9, 10, 11) sts 4 times.

## Sleeves
With smaller needles and MC, cast on 54 (56, 58, 58) stitches. Work in St st,
AT SAME TIME, increase 1 stitch each side every 4th row 14 (14, 14, 17) times,
then every 6th row 6 (6, 7, 6) times—94 (96, 100, 104) stitches.
Work even until piece measures 18 (18½, 19, 20)" from beginning, end with a WS row.

## Shape cap
Bind off 4 stitches at beginning of next 4 rows, 3 stitches at beginning of next 4 rows, 2 stitches at beginning of next 4 (4, 6, 6) rows, 3 stitches at beginning of next 4 rows, 4 stitches at beginning of next 4 rows. Bind off remaining 30 (32, 32, 36) stitches.

## Finishing
Sew shoulders. Set in sleeves. Sew straight edge of side seams, sew sleeve seams. Full as for gauge swatches, using high water setting and 2 TBSP. baking soda and 1/2 cup Ivory soap shavings. When dry, sew pocket linings to pocket extensions on WS of each jacket front.

### Edging
With larger needles and A, cast on 5 stitches. **Row 1** K5. **Row 2** Sl 3 purlwise with yarn in front, k2. Repeat rows 1–2 until edging, slightly stretched, fits around jacket, across lower edges of back and fronts, and along front and neck edges. Bind off. Sew in place. Work edgings for cuffs and pocket openings in same way.

### Embroidery
With tailor's chalk, mark lines for embroidered "knitting needles." With C, work "needles" in stem stitch with satin stitch "knobs." Mark outline for "skein of yarn" on right front. With B, fill in with parallel lines of stem stitch, extending 1" into pocket. Draw spiraling lines for "yarn" across fronts, sleeves and back. With B, work lines in stem stitch. With B, work "knitting" on left front in parallel lines of chain stitch, extending 1" into pocket.

### Buttonholes
Mark placement of buttonholes on right front: the first 1" from top edge, the last 3½" from lower edge, and 3 others spaced evenly between. With sharp scissors, carefully cut 1¼" slits for horizontal buttonholes, starting 1" in from front edge (not including edging). Cut a 24" length of A. Remove 1 ply. Secure buttonholes by working buttonhole stitch around slits and working long stitches at sides. Sew buttons on left front.

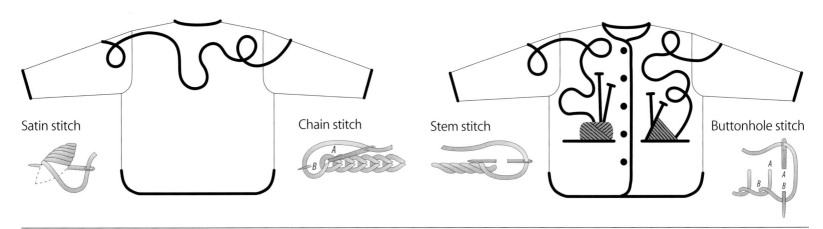

Satin stitch    Chain stitch    Stem stitch    Buttonhole stitch

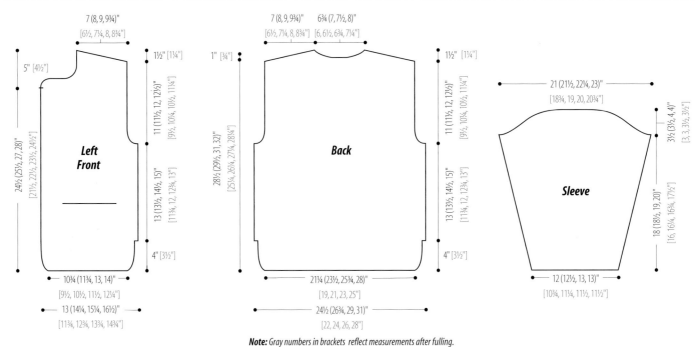

**Note:** Gray numbers in brackets reflect measurements after fulling.

*1* Knit a swatch to pre-felt measurements.

*2* Place in mesh bag (or pillowcase).

*3* Place in washer (with hot water and soap) and agitate...

...checking progress every few minutes.

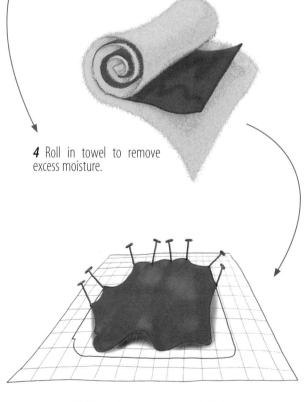
*4* Roll in towel to remove excess moisture.

*5* Pull into shape, measure, and pin to dry... then you are ready for assembly.

# SCHOOL INDEX

## KNIT THROUGH BACK LOOP (k1 tbl)

*1* With right needle behind left needle and right leg of stitch, insert needle into stitch…

*2* …and knit.

## YARN OVER (yo)

**Between knit stitches**
Bring yarn under the needle to the front, take it over the needle to the back and knit the next stitch.

**Between purl stitches**
With yarn in front of needle, bring it over the needle to the back and to the front again; purl next stitch.

**After a knit, before a purl**
Bring yarn under the needle to the front, over the needle to the back, then under the needle to the front; purl next stitch.

**After a purl, before a knit**
With yarn in front of the needle, bring it over the needle to the back; knit next stitch.

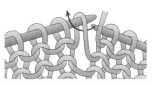

**On next row**
Knit or purl into front of yarn over unless instructed otherwise. The yarn over makes a hole and adds a stitch.

**Yarn over twice (yo2)**
After bringing yarn over the needle (first yarn-over), wrap yarn completely around needle a second time. On next row, work into double yarn-over as instructed.

## INVISIBLE CAST-ON

**A temporary cast-on**
**1** Knot working yarn to contrasting waste yarn. Hold needle and knot in right hand. Tension both strands in left hand; separate strands so waste yarn is over index finger, working yarn over thumb. Bring needle between strands and under thumb yarn so working yarn forms a yarn over in front of waste yarn.

**2** Holding both yarns taut, pivot hand toward you, bringing working yarn under and behind waste yarn. Bring needle behind and under working yarn so working yarn forms a yarn over behind waste yarn.

**3** Pivot hand away from you, bringing working yarn under and in front of waste yarn. Bring needle between strands and under working yarn, forming a yarn over in front of waste yarn. Each yarn over forms a stitch.
Repeat Steps 2–3 for required number of stitches. For an even number, twist working yarn around waste strand before knitting the first row.

## KNIT CAST-ON

**1** Start with a slipknot on left needle (first cast-on stitch). Insert right needle into slipknot from front. Wrap yarn over right needle as if to knit.

**2** Bring yarn through slipknot, forming a loop on right needle.
**3** Insert left needle under loop and slip loop off right needle. One additional stitch cast on.

**4** Insert right needle into the last stitch on left needle as if to knit. Knit a stitch and transfer it to the left needle as in Step 3. Repeat Step 4 for each additional stitch.

## LOOP CAST-ON (ALSO CALLED E-WRAP CAST-ON)

**Often used to cast on a few stitches, as for a buttonhole**
**1** Hold needle and tail in left hand.
**2** Bring right index finger under yarn, pointing toward you.

**3** Turn index finger to point away from you.
**4** Insert tip of needle under yarn on index finger (see above); remove finger and draw yarn snug, forming a stitch.
Repeat Steps 2–4 until all stitches are on needle.

**Left-slanting**    **Right-slanting**

Loops can be formed over index or thumb and can slant to the left or to the right. On the next row, work through back loop of right-slanting loops

## LONG-TAIL CAST-ON

Make a slipknot for the initial stitch, at a distance from the end of the yarn, allowing about 1½" for each stitch to be cast on.
**1** Bring yarn between fingers of left hand and wrap around little finger as shown.

**2** Bring left thumb and index finger between strands, arranging so tail is on thumb side, ball strand on finger side. Open thumb and finger so strands form a diamond.

**3** Bring needle down, forming a loop around thumb.
**4** Bring needle **under** front strand of **thumb loop**…

 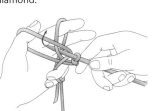 

**5**…up **over index finger yarn,** catching it…

**6**…and bringing it **under** the front of **thumb loop.**

## CABLE CAST-ON

**1–2** Work as for Steps 1 and 2 of Knit Cast-on.
**3** Insert left needle in loop and slip loop off right needle. One additional stitch cast on.

**4** Insert right needle between the last 2 stitches. From this position, knit a stitch and slip it to the left needle as in Step 3. Repeat Step 4 for each additional stitch.

## 3-NEEDLE BIND-OFF

**Bind-off ridge on wrong side**
**1** With stitches on 2 needles, place **right sides together**. * Knit 2 stitches together (1 from front needle and 1 from back needle) (as shown); repeat from * once more.
**2** With left needle, pass first stitch on right needle over second stitch and off right needle.

**3** Knit next 2 stitches together.
**4** Repeat Step 2.
**5** Repeat Steps 3 and 4, end by drawing yarn through last stitch.

## MAKE 1 LEFT (M1L), KNIT

Insert left needle from front to back under strand between last stitch knitted and first stitch on left needle. Knit, twisting strand by working into loop at back of needle.

Completed M1L knit: a left-slanting increase.

## MAKE 1 RIGHT (M1R), KNIT

Insert left needle from back to front under strand between last stitch knitted and first stitch on left needle. Knit, twisting the strand by working into loop at front of the needle.

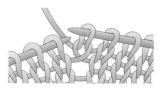

Completed M1R knit: a right-slanting increase.

## MAKE 1 LEFT (M1L), PURL

Insert left needle from front to back under strand between last stitch worked and first stitch on left needle. Purl, twisting strand by working into loop at back of needle from left to right.

Completed M1L purl: a left-slanting increase.

## MAKE 1 RIGHT (M1R), PURL

Work as for Make 1 Right, Knit, EXCEPT purl.

Completed M1R purl: a right-slanting increase.

## S2KP2, sl 2-k1-p2sso

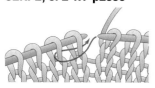

*1* Slip 2 stitches **together** to right needle as if to knit.

*2* Knit next stitch.

*3* Pass 2 slipped stitches over knit stitch and off right needle: 3 stitches become 1; the center stitch is on top.

The result is a centered double decrease.

## SK2P, SL 1-K2TOG-PSSO

1 Slip 1 stitch knitwise.
2 Knit next 2 stitches together.
3 Pass the slipped stitch over the k2tog: 3 stitches become 1; the right stitch is on top. The result is a left-slanting double decrease.

## SSK

*1* Slip 2 stitches **separately** to right needle as if to knit.

*2* Slip left needle into these 2 stitches from left to right and knit them together: 2 stitches become 1.

The result is a left-slanting decrease.

## SSP

*Use instead of p2tog-tbl to avoid twisting the stitches.*

*1* Slip 2 stitches **separately** to right needle as if to knit.

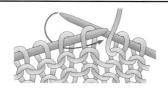

*2* Slip these 2 stitches back onto left needle. Insert right needle through their 'back loops,' into the second stitch and then the first.

*3* Purl them together: 2 stitches become 1.

The result is a left-slanting decrease.

## SSSK

Work same as **SSK** EXCEPT:
*1* Slip **3** stitches....
*2* Slip left needle into these **3** stitches... **3** stitches become 1.
The result is a left-slanting double decrease.

## SHORT ROWS

Each short row adds 2 rows of knitting across a section of the work. Since the work is turned before completing a row, stitches must be wrapped at the turn to prevent holes. Wrap and turn as follows:

**Knit side**
*1* With yarn in back, slip next stitch as if to purl. Bring yarn to front of work and slip stitch back to left needle (as shown). Turn work.
*2* With yarn in front, slip next stitch as if to purl. Work to end.

*3* When you come to the wrap on a following knit row, hide the wrap by knitting it together with the stitch it wraps.

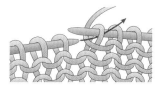

**Purl side**
*1* With yarn in front, slip next stitch as if to purl. Bring yarn to back of work and slip stitch back to left needle (as shown). Turn work.
*2* With yarn in back, slip next stitch as if to purl. Work to end.

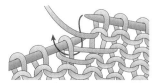

*3* When you come to the wrap on a following purl row, hide the wrap by purling it together with the stitch it wraps.

## BACKWARD SINGLE CROCHET

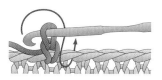

*1* Insert hook into a stitch, catch yarn, and pull up a loop. Catch yarn and pull a loop through the loop on the hook.
*2* Insert hook into next stitch to right.

*3* Catch yarn and pull through stitch only (as shown). As soon as hook clears the stitch, flip your wrist (and the hook). There are 2 loops on the hook, and the just-made loop is to the front of the hook (left of the old loop).

*4* Catch yarn and pull through both loops on hook; 1 backward single crochet completed.

*5* Continue working to the right, repeating Steps 2–4.

### CHAIN STITCH (CH ST, CH)

1 Make a slipknot to begin.
2 Catch yarn and draw through loop on hook.

First chain made. Repeat Step 2.

## 1-ROW BUTTONHOLE

*1* (Right-side row) Bring yarn to front and slip 1 purlwise. Take yarn to back and leave it there. * Slip next stitch, then pass previously slipped stitch over it; repeat from * for each buttonhole stitch. Put last slipped stitch back onto left needle.

*2* Turn work. Bring the yarn to back and cable cast on as follows: * Insert right needle between first and second stitches on left needle, wrap yarn as if to knit, pull loop through and place it on left needle; repeat from * until you have cast on 1 stitch more than was bound off.

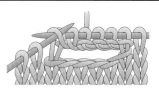

*3* Turn work. Bring yarn to back, slip first stitch from left needle, pass extra cast-on stitch over it, and tighten.

## SINGLE CROCHET (sc)

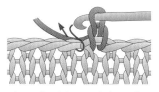

*1* Insert hook into a stitch, catch yarn, and pull up a loop. Catch yarn and pull through the loop on the hook.
*2* Insert hook into next stitch to the left.

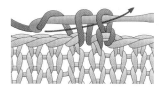

*3* Catch yarn and pull through the stitch; 2 loops on hook.

*4* Catch yarn and pull through both loops on hook; 1 single crochet completed. Repeat Steps 2–4.

## HALF-DOUBLE CROCHET (HDC)

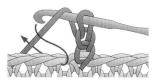

1 Insert hook into a stitch, catch yarn, and pull up a loop. Chain 2 (counts as first half double crochet).
2 Yarn over, insert hook into next stitch to the left (as shown). Catch yarn and pull

through stitch only; 3 loops on hook.
3 Catch yarn and pull through all 3 loops on hook: 1 half double crochet complete. Repeat Steps 2–3.

## I-CORD

Make a tiny tube of stockinette stitch with 2 double-pointed needles:
**1** Cast on 3 or 4 sts.
**2** Knit. Do not turn work. Slide stitches to opposite end of needle. Repeat Step 2 until cord is the desired length.

## GRAFT

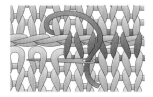

Graft live stitches to rows Compensate for different stitch and row gauges by occasionally picking up 2 bars (as shown above), instead of 1.

## GRAFTING OPEN STS TO CAST-ON EDGE

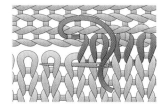

Graft stitches together as shown matching stitch for stitch.

## THREAD SHANK

When sewing on flat buttons, accommodate the thickness of the jacket fabric by making a thread shank. Place a spacer (matchstick, darning needle, or toothpick) across the button and sew over it as you attach the button. Then remove the spacer, bring the needle between the button and fabric, and wrap the yarn around the shank several times before securing with a stitch or two.

## STRANDED 2-COLOR KNITTING

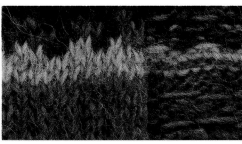

*Right-side and wrong-side of stranded 2-color knitting.*

Two colors worked across a row form a color pattern: the unused color is carried (stranded) along the wrong side of the fabric. These 'carries' should not exceed 1". Weave any carry longer than 1" along the wrong side.

### TIPS
• *Stranded knitting can be worked back and forth (flat) or in the round.*
• *Carries should not be too tight or too loose so as not to affect the gauge or distort the fabric.*
• *Never twist colors between color changes in stranded knitting.*
• *Fair Isle is a style of stranded knitting.*

## 'CUFF-LINK' BUTTON

Give your jacket a dual personality or protect fancy buttons from damage in laundering with 'cuff-link' buttons. Sew two buttons back to back using their own shanks or thread shanks (Steps 1–4). You must make buttonholes on both bands, but the versatility is worth the effort.

*1*  *2*  *3*  *4*

## ATTACHING BUTTONS

• Use a matching thread or yarn to attach buttons (remove a ply from the garment yarn, double it, and sew).
• No button should be wider than the button band.
• For added interest, sew 4-hole buttons onto a jacket using contrasting thread and…
    a plus sign
    an equal sign
    arrows (going every direction)
    boxes
    fill in all directions
…or maybe 2 triangles in a box, a bow tie or hourglass, the letters C, L, N, U, X or Z, or even the number 7.

## BUTTONHOLE PLACEMENT

In ***Jean Frost Jackets***, the left front or left buttonband is worked first, allowing you to work out button placement before you make any buttonholes.

### TIP
*For a woman's garment, adjust button placement so one button aligns with high point of the bust.*

Often you are given specific instructions for placing the top and bottom buttons. To place the remaining buttons evenly between these two, measure the distance and divide by the number of remaining buttons plus 1. If 5 buttons remain, divide the distance (say 15") by 5 + 1; 15 divided by 6 equals 2.5: center a button every 2½".

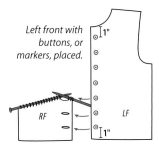

*Left front with buttons, or markers, placed.*

*Right front follows: work buttonholes to match button placement.*

## ZIPPERS

Sewing a zipper into a knit requires care. Although the knitted fabric has stretch, the zipper does not, and the two must be joined as neatly as possible to prevent ripples.
Here are the steps to follow for a smooth zipper placement:

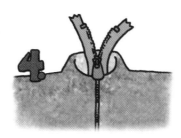

*1* Measure the length of the opening. Select a zipper that matches the length of the opening or is a bit longer.
*2* Pre-shrink your zipper by washing it as you will wash the garment.

*3* Lay the garment flat, making sure that the sides match up.

*4* If you are using a zipper that is too long, align at bottom, allowing extra to extend beyond neck.

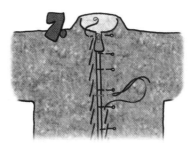

*5* Pin the zipper in place. Be generous with the pins; extra care taken here makes the next steps easier.

*6* Fold under any extra fabric at the top of the zipper and secure with pins.

*7* Baste the zipper in place. When you are satisfied with the placement, remove the pins.

*8* Sew in the zipper, making neat, even stitches.

*9* If the zipper extends beyond the opening, trim extra length.

*10* Reinforce stress points at the top and bottom edges.

## ABBREVIATIONS

**CC** contrasting color
**cn** cable needle
**cm** centimeter(s)
**dec** decreas(e)(ed)(es)(ing)
**dpn** double-pointed needle(s)
**g** gram(s)
**"** inch(es)
**inc** increas(e)(ed)(es)(ing)
**k** knit(ting)(s)(ted)
**LH** left-hand
**M1** Make one stitch (increase)
**m** meter(s)
**mm** millimeter(s)
**MC** main color
**oz** ounce(s)
**p** purl(ed)(ing)(s) or page
**pm** place marker
**psso** pass slipped stitch(es) over
**RH** right-hand
**RS** right side(s)
**sc** single crochet
**sl** slip(ped)(ping)
**SKP** slip, knit, psso
**SSK** slip, slip, knit these 2 sts tog
**SSP** slip, slip, purl these 2 sts tog
**st(s)** stitch(es)
**St st** stockinette stitch
**tbl** through back of loop(s)
**WS** wrong side(s)
**wyib** with yarn in back
**wyif** with yarn in front
**yd(s)** yard(s)
**yo(2)** yarn over (twice)

# specifications:

## Pattern Specifications

| | |
|---|---|
| **INTERMEDIATE**  STANDARD FIT | **Skill level** |
| | **Fit** <br> *Includes ease (additional width) built into pattern.* |
| **Sizes XS (S, M, L, 1X, 2X)** <br> **Shown in Small** <br> *A* 35½ (38½, 41½, 47½, 53½, 56½)" <br> *B* 20½ (21½, 23½, 25, 26, 27)" <br> *C* 27 (28, 28½, 29½, 31, 31½)" | **Sizing** <br> **Garment measurements** <br> *at the A, B, and C lines on the fit icon* |
| 10cm/4" <br>  32 <br> 24 <br> • over Chart pattern <br> using larger needles | **Gauge** <br> *The number of stitches and rows you need in 10 cm or 4", worked as specified.* |
| 1 2 **3** 4 5 6 <br>  <br> • Light weight <br> • 1498 (1605, 1819, 2140, 2568, 2889) yds | **Yarn weight** <br> *and amount in yards* |
|  <br> • 3.75mm/US5 and 4.5mm/US7, or <br> size to obtain gauge, 60cm/24" long | **Type of needles** <br> *Straight, unless circular or double-pointed are recommended.* |
|  <br> • 7 (7, 8, 8, 9, 9) 25mm/1" | **Buttons** |
|  <br> • stitch holders <br> • stitch markers | **Any extras** |
|  <br> **original yarn** <br> RUSSI SALES Heirloom Easy Care 8 <br> (wool; 50g; 107 yds) | **Yarn information** |

## Measuring

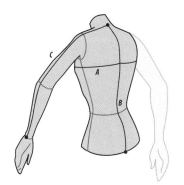

- **A** Bust/Chest
- **B** Body length
- **C** Center back to cuff (arm slightly bent)

## Jacket Fit

STANDARD FIT

LOOSE FIT

OVERSIZED FIT

| bust/chest plus 4–6" | bust/chest plus 6–8" | bust/chest plus 8" or more |
|---|---|---|

## Sizing

Measure around the fullest part of your bust/chest to find your size.

| Women | XS | Small | Medium | Large | 1X | 2X | 3X |
|---|---|---|---|---|---|---|---|
| **Actual bust** | 28–30" | 32–34" | 36–38" | 40–42" | 44–46" | 48–50" | 52–54" |

# at a glance

## Conversion chart

| | | | | |
|---|---|---|---|---|
| centimeters | | 0.394 | | inches |
| grams | | 0.035 | | ounces |
| inches |  | 2.54 | | centimeters |
| ounces | | 28.6 | | grams |
| meters | | 1.1 | | yards |
| yards | | .91 | | meters |

## Needles/Hooks

| US | MM | HOOK |
|---|---|---|
| 0 | 2 | |
| 1 | 2.25 | A |
| 2 | 2.75 | B |
| 3 | 3.25 | C |
| 4 | 3.5 | D |
| 5 | 3.75 | E |
| 6 | 4 | F |
| 7 | 4.5 | G |
| 8 | 5 | 7 |
| 9 | 5.5 | H |
| 10 | 6 | I |
| 10½ | 6.5 | J |
| 11 | 8 | K |
| 13 | 9 | L |
| 15 | 10 | M |
| 17 | 12.75 | N |

## Equivalent weights

| | | |
|---|---|---|
| ¾ oz | | 20 g |
| 1 oz | | 28 g |
| 1½ oz | | 40 g |
| 1¾ oz | | 50 g |
| 2 oz | | 60 g |
| 3½ oz | | 100 g |

## Yarn weight categories

**Yarn Weight**

|  |  |  |  |  |  |
|---|---|---|---|---|---|
| **Super Fine** | **Fine** | **Light** | **Medium** | **Bulky** | **Super Bulky** |

**Also called**

| Sock Fingering Baby | Sport Baby | DK Light-Worsted | Worsted Afghan Aran | Chunky Craft Rug | Bulky Roving |
|---|---|---|---|---|---|

**Stockinette Stitch Gauge Range 10cm/4 inches**

| 27 sts to 32 sts | 23 sts to 26 sts | 21 sts to 24 sts | 16 sts to 20 sts | 12 sts to 15 sts | 6 sts to 11 sts |
|---|---|---|---|---|---|

**Recommended needle (metric)**

| 2.25 mm to 3.25 mm | 3.25 mm to 3.75 mm | 3.75 mm to 4.5 mm | 4.5 mm to 5.5 mm | 5.5 mm to 8 mm | 8 mm and larger |
|---|---|---|---|---|---|

**Recommended needle (US)**

| 1 to 3 | 3 to 5 | 5 to 7 | 7 to 9 | 9 to 11 | 11 and larger |
|---|---|---|---|---|---|

## Yarn substitutions

Throughout this book, the photo caption describes the yarns and colors in the photograph. If a yarn is not available, its yardage and content information will help in making a substitution. Locate the Yarn Weight and Stockinette Stitch Gauge Range over 10cm to 4" on the chart. Compare that range with the information on the yarn label to find an appropriate yarn. These are guidelines only for commonly used gauges and needle sizes in specific yarn categories.

## Contributors

Lily M. Chin

Linda Cyr

Kay Dahlquist

Kim Dolce

Jean Frost

Norah Gaughan

Stephanie Gildersleeve

Lana Hames

Cynthia Helene

Katharine Hunt

Debra M. Lee

Shirley Paden

Charlene Schurch

Barbara Venishnick

Jill Wolcott

Lyn Youll

Kathy Zimmerman